of feeling *tired* all the time?

Tired
of feeling *sick* all the time?

How long
have you suffered *already?*

How much longer
will you *continue* to suffer?

What do you fear
from *more and more* drugs?

Could your life slip away
as you *worsen* every year?

You want more than answers –
you want relief in 100 days!

Advances in "Outside the Box" Treatments
from Best-Selling Author of
THE YEAST SYNDROME

John Parks Trowbridge M. D., FACAM

You lose *every* time you don't try.℠

I need to share this booklet right now with ...

_____

_____

_____

_____

_____

Questions I want to ask so I can get relief:

_____

_____

_____

_____

_____

_____

_____

_____

You lose *every* time you don't try.^{SM}

Find it *now* – Fix it *right!*

Why You *Must Learn More* About THE YEAST SYNDROME

Thirty-one years after publication of this million-copy Best-Seller for Bantam Books, this well-documented and easy-to-read book continues to hold an enviable sales ranking on amazon.com:

    #*18* in Diseases & Physical Ailments/Candida
    #1394 in Alternative Medicine/Healing
    #1948 in Women's Health

The average U.S. *non*fiction book is now selling less than **250** *copies* per *year* and less than **3,000** *copies* over its *lifetime*. Over 300,000 ***new*** titles are published each *year* in the U.S.

"A valuable, timely, and life-enhancing book ... the single information source for everything known to date about a heretofore unrecognized clinical entity – the Candida Syndrome." – Abram Hoffer, M.D., Ph.D., Editor, *Journal of Orthomolecular Medicine*

"I recommend this to EVERYONE who wants to stay healthy or improve their health. Dr. Trowbridge discusses a mostly-unknown epidemic that is responsible for so many illnesses A through Z and is causing havoc in people's lives." – Gayle A. Lighty

"As a caregiver who had to educate herself about candida overgrowth in order to help her father with systemic candida, I can vouch for this particular reference above all the others out there." – Anonymous

"Full of great info and it helped me make sense of some unusual things that were going on." – Kirsten Shaw

You lose ***every*** time you don't try.℠

Because *health* is your greatest *wealth!*

How To Enjoy And Share This Book

First – just **browse** through the pages, stopping where some topic or idea attracts your attention.

Read the stories about how other people have finally found a treatment program that has helped them.

Think of what you could do if you felt better for the days of your life – or maybe if one of your family members was no longer suffering.

Look for explanations that make sense: about how you get sick with The Yeast Syndrome, about how the treatment program is designed to restore your health, about disease changes you want to avoid.

Make your own notes in the margin of questions you have or details you want to remember – or write on pages at the end of the book.

"Dog-ear" pages you want to find easily and refer to often – it's *your* book, use it every day in ways that work best for *you!*

Order your own copy of Bantam Books' best-selling THE YEAST SYNDROME – amazon.com, b&n.com, others – so you have even more details and stories.

And enjoy learning about a brighter future!

You lose *every* time you don't try.[SM]

Find it *now* – Fix it *right!*

Sick and Tired?

Because *health* is your greatest *wealth!*

Find it *now* – Fix it **right!**

Because *health* is your greatest *wealth!*   7

You lose *every* time you don't try.^{SM}

Find it *now* – Fix it *right!*

Ask Nancy

Nancy became all too familiar with colds and "upper respiratory infections" – usually in August and December – so much so that her family doctor remarked on her pattern 15 years ago. And the treatment was always the same: antibiotics until better, cough medications as needed.

If she had "gotten better," then why did she keep "coming down" with another infection? Isn't *that* the most important question that a doctor *should* consider … **and** answer?

Usual things in your world sometimes can turn against you. In 2005, Nancy suffered an asthma episode after being around oak wood smoke all day and then exercising that night. The pulmonary specialist didn't diagnose her condition to be asthma and she remained sick for 6 weeks, not able to breathe fully and noticing a gray "ash" color to her skin. She returned to the lung doctor but was seen by the physician assistant … who offered a breathing treatment. Within 5 minutes, she began to breathe fully. The PA thought this might be "seasonal asthma" and prescribed Advair, which she used for at least a year. She slowly took herself off the drug, thinking she was "all better." Then came again the familiar pattern of August and December illness.

Nancy's husband recommended that she see Dr. T as someone who could focus on here overall health issues. She was "sort of" hopeful after our first meeting. The program of dietary changes, nutritional supplements, and medications aimed at treating The Yeast Syndrome produced welcome improvements within weeks. No longer gaining weight constantly, no longer suffering with frequent illnesses or even stomach viruses – these results convinced her easily.

People rarely realize how "connected" their discomforts might be ... Nancy's long-standing severe back pains when walking or getting in and out of her car slowly faded away, now feeling normal again. She was excited to add our other health-enhancing programs as well, such as bio-identical hormone replacement ("HRT," we've been doing elegantly for over 30 years) and chelation therapy to reduce her body burden of toxic heavy metals.

How does Nancy describe our office? "A customized, detailed health plan is designed for each patient, with a process of tracking changes as well as improvements as lab tests and physical exams are performed. The nurses follow-up often and there's a system for answering questions and concerns in a timely manner. You're not lost in the shuffle! Dr. T and the nurses know what's going on with each patient and in their lifestyle as well."

Find it *now* – Fix it *right!*

Why is Nancy so excited about being a patient here? "I have lots more energy less hair loss, better focus. I don't get shaky with sugar because I stay away from sugar and eat proteins according to my specific diet. I can function well in my very active life. A family member asked what I was doing differently – hair? make-up? or what? – since I seem to have 'de-aged' 20 years!"

Some photos are better to share than those "posters" on the Post Office wall!

You lose *every* time you don't try.℠

Because *health* is your greatest *wealth!*

Quick Questions

What tests have you had that never seemed to make sense to you?

What "diagnoses" have you been offered that never seemed to make sense to you?

Which family members or friends need to hear about these ideas now?

Other answers I am looking to find today:

You lose *every* time you don't try.

Find it *now* – Fix it *right!*

Quick Answers
To Your Urgent Questions

Am I really *sick?* – I feel okay.

Great question – you might be developing problems over many months or years. If you have simple but not obviously nasty symptoms, you could worsen quickly. Your doctors might not have figured out that you have more serious changes coming along.

I have several frustrating symptoms – what could be causing them?

Hardly *anyone* suspects that toxins from an undiscovered yeast "infection" could be causing many problems suffered by many people. Time to take a look.

I *am* really sick – why could my illness be due to The Yeast Syndrome?

Yeasts growing out of control in your gut or sinuses (even elsewhere) can produce poisons that spread throughout your body and gradually wear down your systems.

What is this "yeast," exactly?

We know about bread and beer, but yeast are little *microbes* that live inside *each* one of us – waiting to cause problems when you get stressed by drugs and diet and other challenges in life.

Does *everyone* have this "yeast"?

Yep. But a strong immune system can keep you feeling okay. Antibiotics, cortisone, birth control pills (oral contraceptives), and sugars and starches in a "deplorable" diet can stimulate yeasts to grow out of control.

How can I be sure that yeast is causing *my* problems?

We look for specific problems in your past or present – and we have a couple of blood tests that can help – but *getting better* with a simple treatment program for The Yeast Syndrome can be very convincing.

What tests will I need?

The "best test" is a detailed history, then we get several basic blood and urine tests. Other exams might be useful, depending on your reports.

Why can't I just limit sugars and starches and take some vitamins – do I really need "doctoring"?

Actually, many people feel *much better* with simple dietary changes. If the results you get produce all the improvements you need, that's fine!

The diet has got to be tough – I'm not sure I can do it.

When you feel better with simple changes, you can find it lots easier to eat healthier! The better you get, the more foods are "added back" to your diet, sometimes quickly.

Aren't drugs dangerous? – I don't want to take risks!

We pay attention to the risks because you don't need *more* problems. Remember that drugs to help control the illness problems people can suffer can have risks that are *much* worse than those safer drugs used for treating yeast.

I can't afford to "be sick."

Right! We work to get you feeling better and getting on with your life quickly and easily! Call to talk with us!

Find it *now* – Fix it *right!*

How long before I can feel better?

Surprisingly, most folks feel *lots better* within *weeks* … then steadily improve even more in coming months.

How long will I have to continue with a treatment program?

Your personalized program is designed to produce results as quickly as possible – how well you stay on the program and how easily your body repairs the "damage" are the factors that can take more time or help you get better faster.

Is "the program" the same for everyone?

One size fits *none!* Your program will be custom-tailored to best meet *your* needs.

I can't afford expensive "medical care" for The Yeast Syndrome.

Actually, the most expensive care you can get are treatments that don't work! Most patients no longer need the expensive and risky drugs they might have been on for years, as their problems repair and disappear. Feeling better is always more affordable than staying sick … and getting sicker.

I can't afford the time off to travel for treatment.

No one can! If you are "quite ill" and need up to 2 years to "get all better," you might have 6 or 8 office visits over that time. The more you "stick with your program," the quicker you get results and the longer between office visits.

Can't I find a doctor closer to me for care?

Maybe! Some folks are so sick or so complicated, they might need our specialty expertise (since 1983) – but we're happy if others get you well!

Do I *really* have to read the book and stay on a "program"?

Because *health* is your greatest *wealth!*   15

You're kidding, right? *Our* job is to define the program to help you repair quickly – *your* job is to **learn how to get better quickly and stay well** for *your* future.

Will I have to do a treatment program for the rest of my life?

What you'll need to do is learn and practice healthy living, mostly "eating right" and reducing many of the less obvious risks that challenge us in our daily life.

What about other questions that I have?

How about visiting our office or at least making a call to our Treatment Counselors – or maybe sending an email or a fax or a letter. Contact information is at the end of this book. And you can find many answers on our entertaining website, **www.healthCHOICESnow.com** -- because if you don't *know* that you have health choices *now*, then *you don't have any!*

You lose *every* time you don't try."

Find it *now* – Fix it *right!*

Ask Gary

Happily, Gary is still alive, so you *can* ask him questions! Many of the people with whom he used to work at the refinery have died since the time that he started care with Dr. T. Funny thing, they often ridiculed him for the changes he made in his activities and diet, for the supplements and medications that he took faithfully … *and still does*.

Most people fail to realize how your body systems are interdependent and how worsening in one can lead to collapse in others. Gary found his early problems with The Yeast Syndrome seemed easy enough to control – then, in his early 40s, years of accumulation created toxic overload with heavy metals and organic chemicals (many apparently from his job exposures) finally caught up with him and created severe "adrenal fatigue." Basically, your "stressed-out body" simply can't hold up anymore, even to the simplest demands. Gary couldn't walk 20 yards from his house to his mother's, next door. He took a medical leave for 14 months

How bad was he suffering? He called it "a living hell." An outdoorsman who had enjoyed East Texas to the fullest, he was no longer able to enjoy any activities about which he was passionate. "I felt like a caged tiger in a zoo!"

Where do you start helping someone whose whole body is collapsing as an adult approaching middle age? At the beginning. Sounds easy but managing multi-system disorder requires many years of training, study, and expertise, since the physician has to identify and lay the foundation for recovery, a "first-things-first" approach. Treatment for The Yeast Syndrome was essential, since yeast toxins damage essential biochemical processes across all systems.

Gary needed chelation therapy[1] treatments, FDA-approved programs to reduce his body burden of toxic heavy metals. Since highly poisonous mercury continues to "leach" (trickle out) from so-called "silver fillings," he was referred to a "biological dentist"[2] to remove and replace these with safer dental materials. Coordinating these programs and managing sometimes complex medication and nutritional supplement patterns[3] required special attention by Dr. T and Gary, but motivation to feel better (and to avoid getting worse!) makes the effort easier.

---

[1] Chelation compounds are specially made to "wrap around" or otherwise "grab"

[2] This complicated procedure should be performed by a skilled dentist who has pursued further training and invested in the special equipment needed to protect both the patient, the dentist, and the staff from toxic exposures during the removal. Dr. T served as president of the International Academy of Biological Dentistry and Medicine and is certified in this program except, of course, for the dental procedures.

[3] Dr. T received a Diplomate in Preventive Medicine in 1985 from the Medical Research Institute of the Florida Institute of Technology in Melbourne for master's-level studies in nutritional medicine.

Find it *now* – Fix it ***right!***

Was all this hoopla worth it? Gary notes, "I am an avid bass fisherman, love to hike – never passing up a trail – and now have time to enjoy the outdoors even more, having retired after 38 years with a major corporation." As a delightful side benefit, he returned to work as a consultant 3 months later, able to choose his activities so that they don't interfere with the fun in his life.

As another side note: In 1999, Gary asked whether his left knee, which had been operated several times, could be restored enough for him to resume competitive soccer play. Dr. T had considerable experience with an advanced "prolotherapy"[4] procedure and concluded that repair was likely. Over the next 2-plus years, Gary's treatments allowed his aggressive return to the soccer field until his adrenal collapse in 2003. He boasts that his knee has continued to be stable to this day, surviving a plateau fracture of the tibia (*not good!*) and still "functioning with zero pain." He is now considering our more recent "regenerative medicine" programs to further strengthen his knee and other joints, possibly allowing him to return to competitive

---

[4] "Prolotherapy" uses gentle injections of a solution into the supporting tissues in and around any joint, designed to encourage "proliferation" (regrowth) to strengthen the area, to allow a return to more normal function, often resulting in complete resolution of pain. "Advanced" prolotherapy (which *we* call "Reconstructive Therapy") uses more natural solutions, often more comfortable for the patient while producing desired results. Dr. T was trained 28 years ago in this advanced technique as was certified as a specialist in "orthopedic medicine," treating arthritis and joint injuries, in 1992 by the American Board of Biological Reconstructive Therapy.

Because *health* is your greatest *wealth!*   19

sports at age 58 – "I am excited about the things to come in my life!"

The answer to pollution is simple: do the very best we can to keep our environment safe as we struggle with the demands of progress. But remember ... "non"-polluting electric cars plug in to power lines that come from electric generation plants powered by coal or water or atomic energy, sometimes solar or wind. So we have to be diligent *AND* smart in order to overcome these challenges to our health.

You lose *every* time you don't try.^{sm}

Find it *now* – Fix it *right!*

Why Do I Get *Sick?*

Great – start with a *simple* question! *Not!*

Actually, the answer *is* rather simple, so long as we don't get bogged down in the details for this or that disease. So, in general .....

You get sick because the chemistry inside your body "slips" off of "dead-center," and you actually feel the difference. Think of it like this: your car engine has to feed air and gasoline into each cylinder in what's called the "intake stroke." Then the intake valves close and the piston in each cylinder moves to compress the mixture into a smaller volume (that produces a better ignition). At just the right moment, the spark plug in each cylinder zaps a spark that fires the fuel explosion, which pushes the cylinder down and turns the crankshaft that finally (later!) leads to turning the wheels. "Spent gases" (that have been burned) get expelled and the cycle starts over. Complicated! But actually quite simple.

If any part of the "internal combustion engine" system is out of sync (think: timing or sequence) with the other parts, your car can "run rough." The ignition (spark) timing can be "off," or one or more valves can be loose, or even the air-gas mixture can be "off," any of a thousand things can go wrong. You depend on your mechanic to find it now and fix it right.

When your "chemistry" gets "off" inside you – hundreds of thousands of things can go awry! – then you can feel these changes the same way you might feel your car engine running rough or not developing power.

We call your chemistry "*bio*chemistry," since it's happening inside *living* cells … *you!* A more formal term is "metabolism," which is *all* of what you do when you do *everything* you do inside. Your energy production system (inside each cell, like "jelly beans" called mitochondria) can be suffering, your cell machinery for making pieces you need can be "off," even the machinery for breaking things down when it's time to recycle compounds. (In biology, a compound is just a bigger "molecule" put together from a bunch of pieces of amino acids [from proteins] or sugars or starches or even fats that are strung together to perform a particular job.)

What if these compounds are needed to make other things inside your cells? Or if they are essential for your immune defense system, to protect you against infections? A hundred zillion questions could be asked, and the answer is always the same:
When your metabolism "breaks down,"
you're getting "sick" on the inside … and
you're beginning to have important
functions fail, leading to problems later, like
dominoes falling for months and years.
That *"later"* might even be within a few minutes!

Find it *now* – Fix it *right!*

So here's *all you will need to remember* about **"getting sick"**:

Your body is a marvelous miracle machine, intensely more complicated than a Swiss watch or a rocket engine or the world's smartest computer.

Your body knows how to repair and rebuild when functions are failing – but only if you …

… *remove* things that are **blocking** you from getting better or that are actively causing injury to your metabolism (hint: you can think of infection and toxicity or poisoning) … and

… *provide* essential but **missing** parts, without which you simply can't make the needed repairs (hint: we call this "nutrition" or "proper foods" and "supplements") … and

… *flip* "ON" the **switches** that allow your healing to go forward rather than "stuck-in-stall," waiting for the **GO** signal to make your repairs happen.

See? Pretty simple when you see the big picture.

Now we'll show you how The Yeast Syndrome – and even worse, Deep Blood Fungus – can steal your health and keep you **Sick and Tired!**

You lose *every* time you don't try.^{sm}

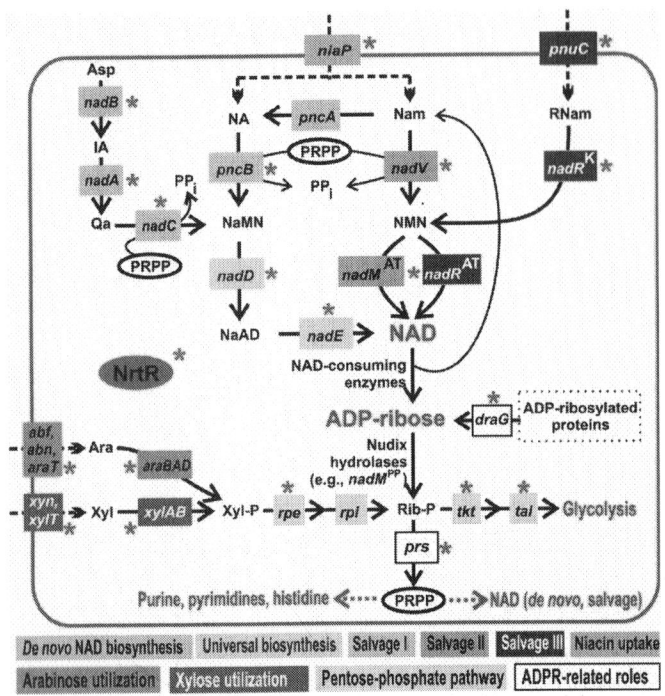

See, it's really pretty simple: Find all the things that are *blocking*, get **rid** of them ….. Find all the things that are *missing*, make sure to **provide** them ….. Find the *switches* that need to be flipped, turn them **on**!

Got that? Good! Now you go to the board and draw that for us – go on, don't be bashful. Everyone makes a mistake or two the first time. After all, that's why we study and review – to be right and to produce wonderful results for patients!

You lose *every* time you don't try.ˢᵐ

Find it *now* – Fix it *right!*

Ask Vosky

A woman aging very gracefully through her middle adult years, Vosky found her health being challenged by the job she loved … but which required frequent travel and stressful days. There simply wasn't any time for digestive problems such as irritable bowel syndrome – bloating, diarrhea then constipation – and frequent need to empty her bladder. With these physical discomforts came skin rashes, body aches, fatigue, recurrent pestering sinus infections. As time went by, it looked to her that there wouldn't be enough time for work as her lingering symptoms consumed more and more of her days … and nights.

Happily, Vosky came in for a consultation and was relieved when I confirmed that most (or even *all*) of her distresses could be related to The Yeast Syndrome. One glitch: the demands of her job made staying on an effective treatment program very challenging.

Hoping that other, perhaps simpler to treat, conditions might still be found, she saw several organ-specific specialists. Once more, their advice and prescriptions failed to produce desired results, just as before. Just like the line in the sand drawn by Jim Bowie at the Alamo, Vosky came to the conclusion that she had to commit to whatever extra efforts she would need to make to get well, working *around* her job duties, even though these efforts left her precious little time for "personal enjoyment" over the next several months.

Whoa, was Vosky in for a surprise! Having committed honestly to changing her diet – to eating meats, eggs, vegetables, and yogurt – to taking her supplements and prescribed medications, and to getting enough rest … her improvements came quickly. She realized that this approach was "cleaning her system from yeast." To boost her progress, we used various IV (intravenous) solutions that restored more normal biochemistry functions more rapidly. Five years after starting, she considers these dietary changes to be simply the lifestyle that promotes and insures her (much) better health. She simply says, "The Yeast Syndrome book was written about me!"

Vosky boasts at looking great because she has slimmed and trimmed, she has boundless energy, and all her body systems work comfortably. Perhaps unexpectedly, she enjoys the challenges of her work so much so that she chooses to take advantage of opportunities to work more so than before. She sleeps well, awakens rested, and dances through her life feeling happy!

You lose *every* time you don't try.℠

Find it *now* – Fix it *right!*

Why Do I Feel *Tired?*

Finally – a *simple* question!

You feel tired because you don't feel energetic and enthusiastic to *do what you want to do*.

(You'd better be smirking right now, since *that* "answer" is *no answer* at all!)

"Tired" is a fascinating symptom, it's one we call "constitutional." If you come in complaining of pain in your right elbow, we focus our attention toward that part of your anatomy. But when you come in with an "all over" complaint – "tired" or "fatigued" or similarly – such a problem is affecting your entire body function, which we call your "constitution."

People who are "tired" (which usually means *"Sick and Tired"!*) can offer a hundred ways to explain it, depending on how they feel and their own experiences:

> drained, fatigued, sleepy, beat, droopy, spent, wasted, worn out, burned out, dog-tired, drowsy, haggard, played out, run-down, tuckered out, and more.

Here's a simple way to look at your problem. Your complaint of "tired" is the **bottom** end of a funnel. The *causes* of your complaint have entered into the **top** end of the funnel from any direction. Simply

Because *health* is your greatest *wealth!*

said: you can feel tired from **any** of a number of **different** reasons – and, to make diagnosis and treatment even more complicated!: you can have two or more reasons to be tired, *all at the same time*.

Let's talk about a table or chair, so you can see how your treatment program **must** work. Many pieces of furniture have **four** legs, giving you stability and safety. You might have "just *one*" leg needing repair … that would be simple. But you want your doctor to help with all of the reasons causing your "tired" problem, not just some of them. So, **all four legs have to be fixed** and working right at the same time. Otherwise, you could continue to be "tired" from any one or two "legs" (or *reasons* in your metabolism) that remains "unfixed" … and then you'll be even more frustrated because seemingly "*nothing* has helped!"

Okay, now you see that "constitutional" complaints – like being "tired" – can have a bunch of different sources, *each one* of which needs to be identified and properly treated. Keep your eye on the prize: **you need to feel energetic and able to do what you want to do!**

The list, however, is *very, very long* … so you'll find a (*short!*) list at the end of the book, organized in a reasonably easy way for you to see why so *many* problems can arise … inside *you!* See the chapter ….. **Why *Could* You Feel Tired?** for a list of Common and Uncommon Causes of Suffering

You lose *every* time you don't try.℠

Find it *now* – Fix it *right!*

Ask Kevin

The early adult years are where you are supposed to feel comfortable if not fantastic. Not so for Kevin, whose 20s, 30s, and 40s were littered with daily diarrhea, cramping, belly bloating, foul-smelling intestinal gas, fatigue, acne, problems with concentration and memory, and persistent cravings for sweets. The tetracycline and other antibiotics his doctors had prescribed had only worsened his symptoms, to the point that Kevin felt his intestines had actually been damaged and might never recover.

Two gastroenterology gut specialists completed a full round of intensive studies, including "scope" exams from top and bottom ("esophago-gastroscopy" and "colonoscopy"), to no avail. A hospital-based specialist and other gastroenterologists were consulted, even a Mayo Clinic specialist. Still, all of his complaints continued without improvement.

A "wholistic" doctor – one who rarely advises drugs or surgery – suggested that Kevin might be suffering with The Yeast Syndrome ... so he made the flight from Colorado to see Dr. T. From the very start, he was unusually hopeful that recovery was within reach, even though the advised dietary program was a bit challenging at first. Taking the prescribed nutritional supplements and then medications was easier than he expected. And then improvements began and continued gradually relieving his discomforts. The severity of his symptoms was so extreme that a medical leave from work made sense, so that he could devote full attention to recovery of the critical functions of his gut and other systems.

Within 3 months, many of Kevin's original complaints – belly cramping pains and bloating, constant diarrhea, gas with a foul intestinal odor – were clearing … results he had never seen before. Since he was feeling more comfortable, the increase in his energy and mental functions was a welcome result as well!

Overall, the daily "sick feeling" that hung over Kevin's waking hours (even awakening him from sleep) has resolved. He has excitedly returned to usual activities and feels able, once again, to participate in his life instead of watching from the sidelines as the years went by. When asked by friends, "Was it worth taking the time and effort and expense to follow your program and travel to see your yeast doctor?" Kevin's answer is simple: "Just do it!"

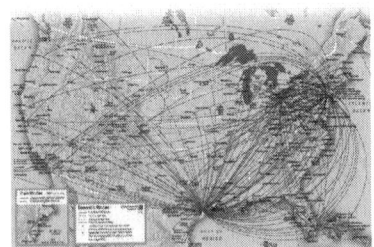

You lose *every* time you don't try.ᔆᴹ

Find it *now* – Fix it *right!*

What Problems *Could* The Yeast Syndrome Create Inside *Me*?

Your question sounds simple enough, since you're used to having the doctor tell you a particular "diagnosis" (what's wrong) and then explain how that can make you feel (symptoms) … or maybe you check further on "Dr. Google."

The list, however, is *very, very long* … so you'll find a (*short!*) list at the end of the book, organized in a reasonably easy way for you to see why so *many* problems can arise … inside *you!* What is key for you to remember is that … The Yeast Syndrome can directly cause or easily lead to many of the "diagnoses" or other reasons for you to suffer with fatigue, with "sickness," with "tiredness."

Remember this key point: yeast and fungi wreak havoc inside your body by interfering at key steps in your metabolism. In other words, they are targeting the very chemistry by which you stay alive … they simply want to make a Happy Meal® out of you! Nothing personal, just business.

Here's an easy explanation so you can understand just how you can get sick with The Yeast Syndrome … and how so many physical (and mental, and emotional) problems can plague you for dozens of years to come.

Because *health* is your greatest *wealth!*   31

First, realize that "yeast" – most often the common one named *Candida albicans* (pronounced like the nation of Canada and rhymes with "Al" – pecans) – has been with human life for eons. Ever since you were a tiny infant, *C. albicans* has grown quietly inside your intestines, your gut.

Most often we find Candida in stool samples, and your colon – your large intestine – harbors more than just this one yeast but many, more than yeast but also other fungi, zillions of bacteria, even viruses and parasites. Those "bugs" or "germs" growing inside us are called our "microbiome." That fancy term simply means the collection of microscopic life forms that make their home in the contents of your gut.

Recent research suggests that the pattern of microbes harbored inside your gut – from your mouth through the end of your colon – dramatically affects the diseases you are likely to develop or already have. Indeed, an abundant overgrowth of such yeasts clearly contribute to damage to your biochemistry and lead to many (maybe most?) of the discomforts and symptoms with which you suffer.

Here's the ominous fact: your lifestyle has an incredible impact on the pattern of bacteria/yeasts/viruses/parasites growing inside you. Antibiotics you receive for any reason can kill numbers of bacteria in your gut, some of which will never return and regrow inside you, and that permanently alters the balance of organisms inside. A variety of other drugs – such as

Find it *now* – Fix it *right!*

cortisone (corticosteroids) and certain hormones, particularly for birth control and menopause, alter the pattern as well.

More worrisome, on a daily basis, is that your selection of foods – especially refined sugars and starches, processed and preserved and packaged foods – can have a dramatic and steadily worsening impact on your gut "bugs" (which we call "flora and fauna," loosely plants and animals).

A number of other lifestyle "habits" can influence your microbiome toward the direction of ill health: insufficient sleep, inadequate quality of sleep, overwhelming stress (just daily life can provide this!), exposure to toxic metals and chemicals, limited physical activity, even emotional outlook such as struggling to find a sense of meaning and value in life. Anxiety and depression clearly affect your chemistry and alter your gut bugs. Other infections, illnesses, and environmental challenges (even poor indoor or outdoor air quality) can direct the pattern of your but microbes toward ill health.

Some people ask whether "genetics" might play a role. The set of genes that you get from each parent certainly can limit your physical and even mental capabilities. Scientific studies would suggest that your "health habits" (as outlined above, including your faith in the future) have a far greater impact on the microbial life harbored in your gut.

So here's the real answer: the "bugs" growing in your gut put out a variety of "waste products" that your body can absorb along with the water and minerals from your colon. The molecules produced by Candida have been documented to poison specific areas of your biochemistry. Indeed, their effects are to interrupt chemical reactions that you need for healthy function … so we call these "Canditoxins." Never be fooled: these are poisons!

To make it simple for you to see where dozens and dozens of symptoms (discomforts that only you can feel, such as a headache) and signs (changes that we can see or measure "from the outside," such as a fever or a rash), consider the example of traffic congestion.

To block all the cars and trucks from coming into Florida from the Florida Keys, all you need to do is put some sort of roadblock on that road, US Hiway 1, heading toward Miami. That's the *ONLY* highway coming onto the mainland from the Keys. Indeed, traffic could back up all the way to Key West, unless and until the roadblock is removed.

Another great example is to consider how many cars or trucks need to be "disabled" (by an accident or mechanical problem) in order to bring traffic on all of Houston's roads to a standstill. Perhaps as many as 20 "roadblocks" – such as fender-bender accidents all within the area surrounded by the Loop (I-610) – would soon bring

Find it *now* – Fix it *right!*

all movement to a halt. First, the major roads would slow down and stop, then finally all of the smaller streets and even alleys. *No one* would be able to drive anywhere.

Think of the "slowing traffic" as your body developing various illnesses … then when the traffic grinds to a stop, that's when you become more severely limited by disease. The impact of these identified yeast poisons cannot be underestimated. I call the chemical reactions where these toxins interfere as "pinch points" in your metabolism – these are the key "intersections" on your internal "road map" where blockages can do overwhelming damage to your health.

Most physicians have no idea about the many problems and the ominous illness issues associated with yeast and particularly *Candida albicans*. Now you have critical insights that can save your life and the health and lives of your family and friends. So share this information often and widely – they will not hear anything like this from their own doctors, even specialists.

To get a good grasp on the symptoms that could plague you, your family, your friends, turn to these chapters at the end of this book: **Finding Answers In THE YEAST SYNDROME Bantam Books Best-Seller** *and* **What Symptoms *Could* The Yeast Syndrome Create Inside You?**

You lose *every* time you don't try.^{SM}

Quick Questions

What tests have you had that never seemed to make sense to you?

What "diagnoses" have you been offered that never seemed to make sense to you?

Which family members or friends need to hear about these ideas now?

Other answers I am looking to find today:

You lose *every* time you don't try.ᔆᴹ

Find it *now* – Fix it *right!*

Ask Katy

Frustrated with her daughter's belly bloating, mood disorder, longstanding depression, anxiety, and racing brain, Katy's mother insisted that she come in for evaluation. Medications from other doctors failed to produce any results, and our intake forms clearly showed that she was suffering with The Yeast Syndrome. So, I designed a treatment program for starters.

Katy came back in a month, noting that she felt amazing, maybe 100% better. Two months later, with her program beginning to address The Yeast Syndrome, her results were nothing short of amazing. Her husband was pleased, especially because she stated, "I feel like me." She felt so much better that she "disappeared" for almost a year. When she returned with worsening belly pains, nausea, and vomiting, she was suffering with gallstone symptoms. Minor modifications of diet and supplements quickly provided relief. So ..... she "disappeared" again, for over a year.

When Katy came back, she wanted treatment for a worrisome skin abscess (boil) not improving with treatment elsewhere. She quickly got better and then ... yes ... she "disappeared" for a year-and-a-half. She presented suffering from the stress of raising teenagers but her symptoms alarmed her: episodes of feel "hot" and "flushed," leading to markedly elevated heartbeat, tremors and shaking, dry mouth, weakness in her arms and legs, even shortness of breath and severe exhaustion. Clearly her diagnosis was of "autonomic dysfunction," or imbalance in her automatic go/slow nervous system functions.

Referral to a neurologist yielded no further details beyond confirming her "dysautonomia" (another name for autonomic imbalance), but happily specialized nutritional supplements and minimal medications had resolved much of her distress within 3 weeks. Some 3 months later, Katy was struggling with worsening symptoms after she had gotten off her supplements for testing by an endocrinologist. Frustrated with continuing problems, she … yes … disappeared for another year.

On her return to office, Katy agreed to restart a personalized nutritional program – and to restart treatment for The Yeast Syndrome that had never really gotten underway. Results were slow to come, taking over 3 months for various discomforts to lessen. Mildly excessive levels of toxic heavy metals suggested that chelation therapy treatments to reduce their interfering effects (especially in the nervous system) made sense. Indeed, over the following 10 months, Katy continued to show steady symptom improvements. A brief recurrence of her infected skin abscess caused alarm but aggressive antibiotics then probiotic bacteria to rebalance her gut easily controlled the problem.

Find it *now* – Fix it *right!*

So what does the world hold for Katy now? Occasionally she has issues with sleep, with muscle tension, and with headaches … but these discomforts are easily controlled. As she says, "I feel great today – about 98%." Is a commitment to proper eating, to specially prescribed supplements, to occasional medications worth the effort and expense to Katy. I'll let you guess.

What so many people – the general public, even patients undergoing treatment for The Yeast Syndrome – is that the interference in chemical reactions all throughout the body can lead to an incredible number of different symptoms. Literally 10 people could "show up," each with completely different symptoms, and each of them could be diagnosed with – and respond to personalized treatment for – The Yeast Syndrome.

Many people want to "make sense of it all" and are reluctant to pursue responsible treatment until something "clicks" inside their head. Actually, most of today's physicians have exactly the same view: until this all makes sense to me, it can't be real. Sadly, tens of *millions* of patients in the United States are suffering needlessly. One of the reasons we have such incredibly high medical expenses and still suffer with so many problems is ….. because treating anything *other than* the real problem doesn't work!

You lose *every* time you don't try.^{sm}

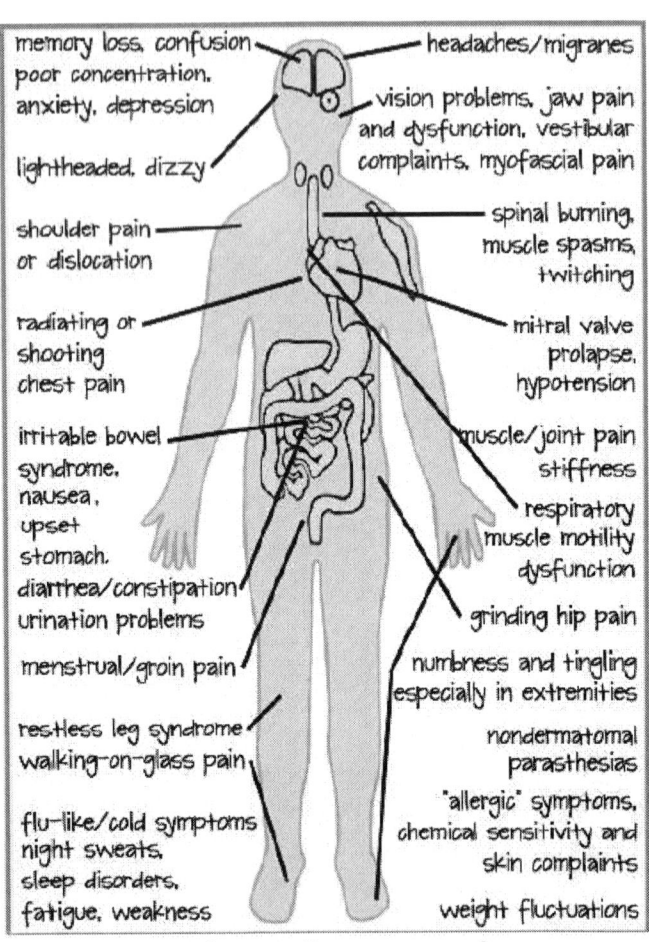

"Disparate" symptoms of
Dysautonomia

Looks a lot like … The Yeast Syndrome

You lose *every* time you don't try.^{SM}

Find it *now* – Fix it *right!*

What Kind Of Specialists Treat The Yeast Syndrome?

Ooops! Another question that needs a detailed answer, so the details you want are listed toward the end of this book.

Ask your specialists about treating your puzzling problems, especially the ones that have lasted *"forever!"* or for which you're having to take continuous medications … or more drugs each year.

Why should you worry about the laundry list of side effects possible with prescriptions that you have to take often or even all the time? Remember your problems start with interrupting your "metabolism" – that's *all* of what you do when you do *everything* you do inside.

When something is going awry inside you – you're *"Sick and Tired"!* – you will live longer and happier and feel better if you get the *causes* corrected, the problems fixed, so that you need fewer drugs or none at all. Medications might help to get your biochemistry fixed – along with nutritional supplements and other needed treatments – but long-term use *can* cause problems for you.

Medications are "stoppers" – they "stop" things from happening inside, they block chemistry that makes you feel uncomfortable. We have antihistamines (allergies), anti-acids (heartburn), anti-hypertensives (blood pressure), anti-inflammatories (pain and swelling), and so on. Pretty soon it becomes obvious that you appear to have an ... "anti" doctor!

Here's a critical question: Can you really *blame* your doctor?

Eager folks start medical school with an idea of helping others recover from injuries and illnesses. Their training focus is on pathology (what goes wrong) and pharmacology (drugs to "stop" what's going wrong or feeling uncomfortable) and surgery (operations to remove or "replace" offending parts).

But ... you are **not** made of drugs or new plastic and new steel. You're not made to be "plumbed differently," all or your parts started in the correct order (exceptions: genetic issues or injuries).

Your doctors are not specifically trained to help your problems "*get* better" or even "go away" with nutritional supplements and dietary changes. You're expecting them to advise you in ways they've not been educated to do. So it's easy to understand when you don't get what you want and what you need for better health.

Find it **now** – Fix it **right!**

R. Stanton Avery, who invented the labels we stick onto envelopes and folders, said it simply: "You're always down on what you're not up on."

So ... be kind to any of your doctors who simply don't have a clue.

But be kind to yourself as well: find the doctors or other "health practitioners" who are trained and experience in helping people to resolve such problems, to finally regain and maintain better health.

One more thing: please share your experiences on your journey to feeling better with all the other people in your circle of friends and family – including folks in your social clubs and church – so that they too can quickly grab a shortcut to recovering their health as well.

For a listing of physicians who could help you to get better with The Yeast Syndrome, check out one of the later chapters in this book: **What Kind Of Specialists *Could* "Treat" The Yeast Syndrome?**

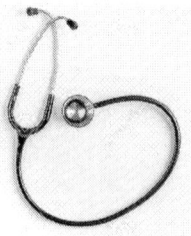

You lose *every* time you don't try.[SM]

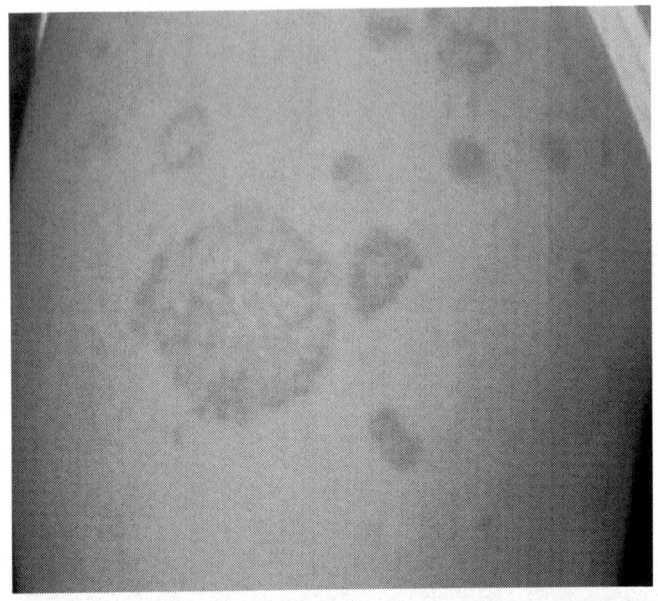

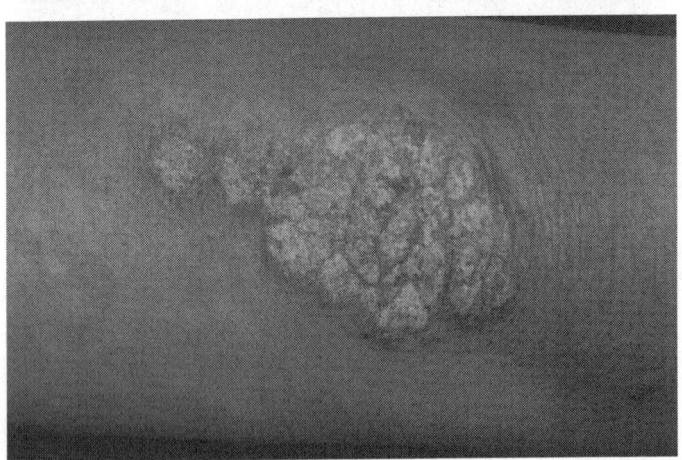

You lose *every* time you don't try.^{SM}

Find it *now* – Fix it *right!*

Ask Mike

Symptoms unknown to many people plagued Mike almost daily: almost disabling belly pains for 6 years, fatigue for over 4 years, recurrent strep throat yearly or more often, headaches since childhood, psoriasis skin rashes as well. A variety of treatments by general doctors, family practice specialists, and a bevy of gastroenterology gut specialists failed to provide any lasting relief.

Frustrated but committed to finding a solution, Mike was told by a friend that many of his problems might relate to "yeast." He found a book called **The Yeast Connection**, scored high on the test inside, and excitedly contacted Dr. Billy Crook, the author, a pediatric allergist in Tennessee. Dr. Crook referred him to Dr. T, whom he had trained starting in 1983. Detailed office forms took a few hours to complete, since he had suffered with so many problems that escaped diagnosis by some 15 doctors over the years. At the conclusion of his first visit with Dr. T, he was excited and optimistic that major improvements were just around the corner.

Critical to Mike's program were a restrictive diet – especially avoiding foods containing sugars and starches – and a set of nutritional supplements to help repair and restore more normal functions in body systems that had been limping along all this time. When yeast-control prescriptions were added, he noticed a remarkable improvement in his feeling of health and wellbeing, one he had not experienced in his entire adult life. Within a couple of weeks, his psoriasis splotches began to resolve, energy improved, and belly pains decreased.

Still true to his commitment to avoid foods that create his discomforts, Mike has been thrilled that fatigue, strep throat infections, and irritated and ugly patches of skin psoriasis have completely disappeared. Only rarely does he notice belly pains, much like almost everyone. Enjoying exceptionally good health, Mike stays in shape by training for – and completing! – *12* marathons. For the first time in his life, he knew from his positive results in every system that he had found the right approach to restore his health.

Mike has followed this life-restoring program for 33 years now. He encourages everyone to realize that no one has to continue to suffer. Mike's advice to people suffering with lingering problems despite the best of traditional care but still reluctant to place their faith in a program that sounds too simple: keep an open mind when conventional care hasn't produced results you deserve, stick with it, and you'll very likely get better.

RUN BABY RUN

You lose *every* time you don't try.^{SM}

Find it *now* – Fix it *right!*

We Three Kings ...

The Christmas story includes a narrative about the Three Kings from the Orient, who come following yonder star in search of the Baby Jesus.

Your journey to recovering and maintaining your health involves ***three kingdoms***. Again, a simple concept will give you a great deal of power in making the best decisions for your recovery.

These 3 kingdoms are the groups of "living organisms," divided according to the chemistry involved in how they gain the energy needed to stay alive. Remember that everything you do inside – your metabolism, all the compounds and chemicals that you make and break down, all the processes that you do every second, every minute, every day of your life – involves energy. An overly-simplified explanation makes all of this easy to see.

Plants, using the green chlorophyll in their leaves, convert sunlight into packages of energy called glucose (sugar). ***Animals*** eat plants to get that energy for themselves – or eat other animals who have eaten the plants. Members of the ***fungus*** kingdom eat both plants and animals in order to get their energy.

Of these 3 kingdoms, the fungi (pronounced "fun' – jy") have to be the "smartest," since they have to overcome any and all defenses put up by plants or animals in order to "eat" them and get the needed energy. Simply this: they want to make a Happy Meal® out of us, out of all animals, out of all plants, especially the dead and dying ones.

When you pause to think about the situation, you realize that yeasts, molds, mildews, and fungi are all members of the fungus kingdom … and they are *all over* your environment. Everywhere!

So your body is constantly under attack and your defenses are forever battling against these "invaders" who are intent on recycling … ***you!***

How easy it is to understand why you can suffer with *so many symptoms* and can be attacked by *so many diseases* – fungi (and bacteria as well) simply look you over with "happy eyes." And then start to take you down.

Take Home Message:
Yeast is a fungus
and you are
just a Happy Meal®.

You lose *every* time you don't try.ˢᴹ

Find it *now* – Fix it *right!*

Choose Your *Health* Care
Like Your Life Depends On It

Too many times our choices regarding "getting better" are based on what pill or potion or operation that might *quickly* help you to "feel better."

Although we've had patients travel from all continents except Antarctica, the stories we hear sometimes are so sad:

"Couldn't you have an office in my part of Houston?" – No.

"My local doctor says that he/she can do whatever you are doing." – What books has your local doctor written? What lectures has your doctor given around the United States or overseas?

"I really don't want to drive that far or take that much time." – Most everyone would be happy to drive to M.D. Anderson for cancer-care or to Texas Heart for specialized surgery … but they often don't realize that enjoying daily comfort and capability as years go by can make a world of difference in life.

"My local doctor says his/her treatments work just as well as whatever you do." – So please ***help me to understand*** … why are you ***still*** sick and tired … and taking various medications? How's *that* working for you? Research often makes a difference!

Because *health* is your greatest *wealth!*   49

"I'm waiting for insurance to pay for your services." – Do you have a rocking chair and can you play checkers or BINGO, so you can pass the years in your nursing care facility?

"I really don't believe that your treatments could help me that much." – Don't confuse you with the *facts*? The only one who still suffers is ... *you*.

"My husband/wife says that doctors like you just make phony claims and take everyone's money but you're not a 'real doctor.'" – Come to our office, sit for a few minutes with our patients, hear their stories, decide for yourself. Check the diplomas on the wall. Read the 60-plus **Who's Who** entries.

"I don't want to spend that much – I have to keep my [rental houses][stock investments][CDs] [savings] for retirement." – Are you aware that *nursing homes* charge about $4,000 *or more* each **month** – and federal and state laws provide for them to lay claim to your assets until you have only a pittance left, apparently *then* you could qualify for Medicaid to pay the nursing care bills.

The *very worst* "excuse" that we hear is this: "I'm doing pretty well right now, I'll come see you when I need you." – Nice thought. But *those* folks unexpectedly end up with worsening illness problems, finally hopping on to the *medical* merry-go-round, with test after test and specialist after specialist.

Find it *now* – Fix it *right!*

Expenses for drugs and surgery can mount up suddenly, insurance deductibles are enormous, continuing care devours your time and your money … and then you don't have *any* funds or energy to seek effective *health* care *here*.

Just maybe … taking time to learn how we might help you as much as we help most others whom we accept for care makes sense. Comfort and capability allow you to experience a joyful life.

For details on Dr. T's professional background and expertise, check out his curriculum vitae at

www.healthCHOICESnow.com/CV   or scan …

How did we choose the name for our website: **healthCHOICESnow**? To us, it's obvious: When you don't *know* that you *have* health choices *now*, then *you don't have any!*

We want you to go where you feel most comfortable with fees and services and all other reasons that are important to you. If you are accepted for care here, we will deliver our very best – always!

Our logo is an astronaut within a heart:

NASA pushed the limits of our understanding in *all* areas of science to design a spacesuit for survival in the hostile environment of outer space. We have never lost an astronaut on a spacewalk.

Our body is the "suit" we depend on every minute of every day. At **Life Celebrating Health**, we push the limits of our understanding in *all* the biological sciences, nutrition, *and* pharmacology in order to help our patients survive in the hostile environment of planet earth.

So much more goes into *healing* care than *medical* care, which some experts feel does little more than simply *respond* to your complaints and

Find it *now* – Fix it *right!*

control your symptoms. Indeed, drugs (and surgery) used in conventional care can create their own serious issues needing special attention.

Once again, honestly ask yourself these questions that are critical for your healthy future:

Sick
of feeling _tired_ all the time?

Tired
of feeling _sick_ all the time?

How much longer
will your doctors _miss_ the diagnosis?

What else will go wrong?

What do you fear
from *never* getting well?

You want more than answers –
you want relief!

**The Yeast Syndrome
could be your
key
to a healthier, happier,
more delightful future.**

You lose *every* time you don't try.™
Because *health* is your greatest *wealth!*   53

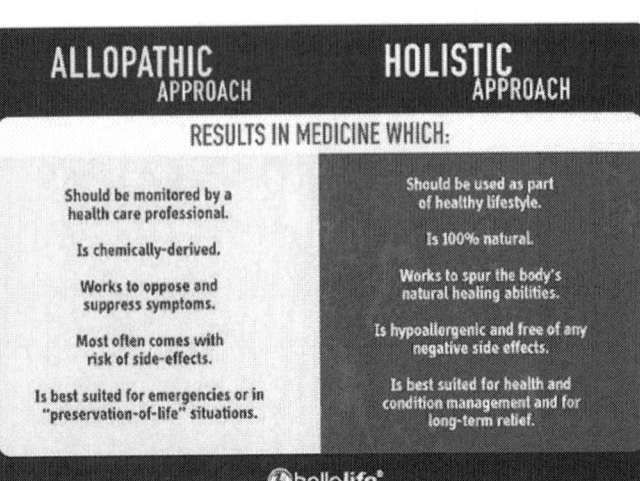

"Allopathic" = *conventional* medical care
"Holistic" (Wholistic) = *whole person*/natural care

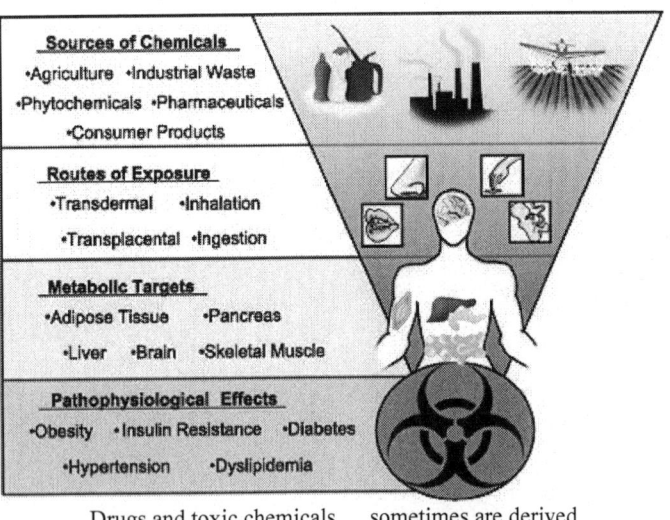

Drugs and toxic chemicals ... sometimes are derived
from the "*same*" sources – *and both* have adverse effects.

You lose *every* time you don't try.[SM]

Find it *now* – Fix it *right!*

Ask Kelly

Pause for a moment, take a deep breath, and praise God that your problems are hardly as severe as those that limited Kelly's life for years. Her symptoms were exceptional – but almost everyone knows someone who has suffered a lifetime of distresses that have never improved despite the efforts of dozens of doctors.

Where could Kelly start to describe her many complaints? Belly bloating and diarrhea were constant companions, as were teeth and gum pains and daily hoarseness. Brain fog blurred her concentration and memory, ringing in her ears never left, draining fatigue and headaches and disturbing changes in her vision lingered despite any attempted treatments. Many days she had to wear sunglasses indoors, just to tolerate her eyes being open. Skin peeling and overall itching were frustrating, but muscle aches were painful. Losing her hair looked like a minor problem in light of her feeling cool or even cold all the time. Where could Kelly turn, she felt she had looked literally everywhere.

To say that getting to feel better was easy for her would be unfair to any reader. When so many body systems have suffered such profound disruptions to normal function, the road to improvement is more of a determined dance … first get these symptoms lessened, then pay attention to these others, then focus more on certain others, and so on. Kelly was thrilled that Dr. T was always willing to take the time to listen, to figure out and then carefully explain the next steps along the way. That reliable partnership kept her committed to the long term program she required to restore the underlying healthy balance of her systems.

How does Kelly feel now? "I have gone from sitting in my recliner week after week to staying busy from morning to later evening." She does all this on 6 to 7 hours of sleep rather than 10 or more she used to need, just to get by. "I'm thrilled that my old shoulder and hip injuries have improved to where they are only slightly irritated, and I have the energy of a 30 year old." Not bad for a middle-aged adult, working fulltime! "I've started playing the piano regularly again, after 30 years … despite starting college with a piano scholarship, but the yeast brain-drain caused me to give it up." Kelly notes that her recovery allows her once again to feel the great joy of making music. "I can finally feel the electrical current connecting across the empty spaces in my brain. Thanks to my piano practice, I can feel myself getting smarter and loving it!"

Kelly almost forgets to mention the dramatic improvements she has realized with the many other physical symptoms that kept her life bound down for so many years. When pressed for details, she notes with a chuckle that her skin is now sensitive again to touch rather than diminished as before. She can tilt

Find it *now* – Fix it *right!*

her head side to side without becoming dizzy. All thoughts of having to give up her job have been replaced by thoughts of working for several more years. Kelly is excited to find simple solutions to tasks that had frustrated her for years, such as organizing storage in her garage. Muscle control and balance is better, and she's able to get up from the floor more comfortable when doing yoga. All better? – not yet. But her life is going in the "right direction" after years of failing health: "Changes and progress are coming faster now."

When you think of "unrelated" medical problems, you might win by thinking of how treatment for The Yeast Syndrome could contribute to complete healing. Especially in diabetics.

As an example, consider the frustration suffered by people with "peripheral neuropathy" (altered sensations in feet and legs), foot ulcers, chronic venous stasis ulcers, even cracked heels or soles (skin breakdowns that "refuse" to heal). For many of these patients, treatment has been successful by carefully combining anti-fungal medications for The Yeast Syndrome along with antibiotic medications for bacterial infections, nutritional supplementation for skin/blood vessel healing, dietary changes to support healthy tissues, supplemental oxygen to boost healing capability, chelation therapy to reduce interference by toxic heavy metals, stem cell treatments that boost healing patterns, even hormones that encourage tissue repair. (Maybe even a little voo-doo if needed as well?) Saving life and limb sometimes requires expertise far beyond usual thinking and training.

Take a moment to realize that diabetes mellitus is a disease where your blood sugar rises above normal. Since yeast and fungus devour sugars (and starches), conditions like diabetes (or pre-diabetes, where sugar management becomes irregular) can encourage The Yeast Syndrome to "take hold," especially if other factors (antibiotics, cortisone, and so on) are present. Pre-diabetes is also known as Metabolic Syndrome, a real "heartache" since that's a path toward heart attack and strokes. In "the big picture," so many of our illness problems are interrelated – which means that taking care of The Yeast Syndrome could solve or improve many other illness issues as well!

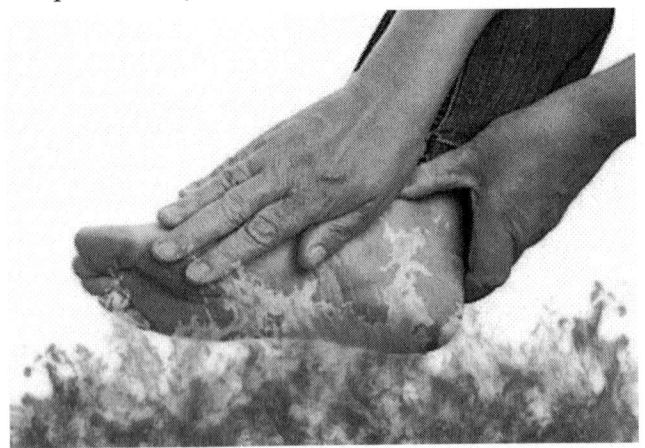

You lose *every* time you don't try.^{SM}

Find it *now* – Fix it *right!*

Kick The Tail Of The One-Trick Pony

Extreme changes in society, insurance programs, and medical practice itself have led not just to focus on the particular kinds of diseases for which doctors feel most comfortable or most rewarded. Rather than helping find the solution *you need*, many can assume that you need the solution *they have*. Whatever happened to old-fashioned doctoring the whole person? Often not *there*.

I used to think that we go to college to learn how to learn. Then we go to medical school to put on valuable blinders, allowing us to focus on the topics of human health and disease, so we could gain viewpoints and experience to help people recover. Then we go to specialty training – residency and fellowship, after medical school – to confine our view through a microscopic lens, learning everything worth knowing about a specific organ or system or disease process.

Sadly, then I learned that specialty training sometimes resembles putting on a pair of eye patches: "Don't confuse me with the facts, I already know what you have and what I'm going to do."

General doctors expect that they can help what you've got. Specialists expect that you have what they can help. Not always – but the results seem to speak for themselves, since patients suffering with discomforts and diseases related to The Yeast Syndrome often have seen 18 or more doctors before they finally find someone who understands the cause of their problems and proposes treatments that work.

What sets us apart at **Life Celebrating Health** is our intense commitment to … *your health*.

Dr. T insists on results and expects you to become an educated partner in your recovery, so that you can *continue* to feel better for years into *your* future.

Your job is to share your concerns and discomforts, **our** job is to figure out what is amiss and how to return you to a healthier, happier life. Some folks have called us a "one-stop shop" for "fixing most everything" in your body. What has

Find it *now* – Fix it *right!*

surprised so many of our new patients is how quickly they can recover from so many different problems.

Dr. T is recognized as a world authority for his skill in diagnosing the root cause of problems sometimes missed by major medical centers for years – then designing treatments that provide impressive improvements in just 3 months or so. That's why our simple slogan is … "Find it *now* – Fix it *right!*"sm

Sadly, many people hope for instant results (a "quick-fix") and they'll listen to almost anyone – trained physician or not – who crows a convincing promise. (That's why internet ads for modern "snake-oil" miracles can make their promoters rich within weeks or months.) Unfortunately, the insurance system often limits your choices to a small set of doctors – but Doctor A is not Doctor B, and Illness A is not Illness B, and the specialty care *you* need is whatever doctor or approach that truly finds the *cause* of, and *fixes*, *your* problems.

Many folks call our office, some shopping for particular treatments or bargain services. While they certainly have problems that need fixing, they impose their own ideas on what testing or treatment they think they "need" and what they are willing to "spend." There are clinics everywhere who will gladly cater to those people. Sadly, the "results" they provide might really "miss the mark."

When there is no existing or effective treatment for a disease or condition, it is easy to understand why you might be blinded by hope and feel you have nothing to lose from trying something new, even if it isn't proven to the general medical community.

At **Life Celebrating Health**, we are very aware of how desperate you can be to find relief and feel better. That's why everyone who is *accepted* as a patient, for whatever reason, receives our intensely personal attention. One key fact to remember: many of the medications (or even operations) advised for problems not recognized as being caused by The Yeast Syndrome can have very serious side effects. *That*, in our opinion, is simply ***not safe***.

We definitely "do it different" from other offices. We have one question for you to answer now: If doctors and patients keep repeating the *same* treatments that didn't work before, why should they expect different results with the next one or the next one after that? After all, how's *that* working for you?

Our testing and treatment approach is based on simple guidelines:
      Safety – *first and always!*
      Results – otherwise, why are we doing it?
     And *then* …   **Comfort**
                      Convenience
                      Cost-consciousness.

                  Find it ***now*** – Fix it ***right!***

Cost of care is *never* "the" major concern, since that would limit what might be the very best approach or treatment to finally resolve your problems. We seek to *safely produce results* for you the same way we would for our family: *that's* our **family standard of care**.

Correct diagnosis is *critical*; correct treatment is *essential*. Dr. T studies your history details, examines you (sometimes a patient is amazed that he actually lays hands on your body when other doctors didn't), and orders specific tests, all seeking to reveal the root causes of your problems.

Treating *where* your problems arise allows your body to do the natural healing that each and every one of us receives as a birthright from God. Sadly, many people unknowingly trade away this precious gift for a "bowl of porridge" that we now call drugs and surgery, and they often go through life miserable. [Remember that Esau sold his firstborn inheritance, his birthright, to younger brother Jacob for a bowl of lentil soup and bread, squandering his life and forever failing to appreciate his remarkable blessings from God. Genesis 25:29-34.]

Through extensive training and dozens of years helping patients heal and teaching other doctors his perspectives, Dr. T has gained the skills to "juggle" the many (and often ignored, unseen, undiagnosed, untreated) factors that need his professional attention in order for your body to mend.

[Here's an exciting little secret: every year, Dr. T discovers newer "twists" to add to our already excellent programs. Even better: some of these discoveries consist of utterly novel approaches, never before introduced into practice. If you had a few hours, you could ask Dr. T to explain what startling information he has found out about yeast and fungus in the past 3 years.]

Back to juggling the many details that are essential for you to get results as expected – *whole* person (*wholistic*) medical and health care:

Remember that "close" counts only in horseshoes, hand grenades, and shotguns. Why trust your wellbeing to someone with less than world-class expertise?

Find it *now* – Fix it *right!*

We take our responsibilities seriously because suffering doesn't just ***run*** your life, it ***ruins*** your life.

Look to become ***partners*** – you do **your part** of *doing* the advised treatment program and *reporting* clearly your results … and we do **our part** of continuing to *search* for ever-better answers to finally resolve your concerns.

After all, what price do people pay to find some comfort in their lives? ***Unless an effective treatment is found***, some folks turn to daily alcohol, others find that drugs and alcohol help blunt the pain, sadly a few choose addicting medications that change their lives in unspeakable ways. Everyone suffering with chronic or frequent daily illness discomforts will experience a change in personality: anger, fear, frustration, loss of patience, loss of enthusiasm, even loss of hope. Disrupting relationships and lives seems a terrible price to pay when relief might literally be close within your reach.

In "the old days," we used to fear dying. Now, we fear getting sick. One major illness or just the treatments for it can cripple your activities, paralyze your optimism, and literally steal your assets and bankrupt your family.

Illness and aging changes can sneak up to the point where discomforts and limitations can steal any chance for restful sleep – and getting going each day or lasting through the day can become an increasing challenge and a daily worry.

Take just a moment to consider a few dozen years of your life: growing up is fun and mostly has few problems; getting older is when we learn to ignore "stuff"'; as time goes by ... hasn't the time come to restore better functions in your body?

When you were younger, recall that you felt comfortable and could move reasonably well. You didn't feel limited or fearful with illness. And you expected to do so for the rest of your life. Well, *today* is the *first* day of the rest of your life. *Let's get crackin'!*

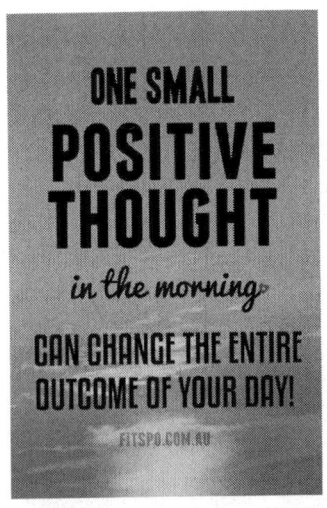

Find it **now** – Fix it **right!**

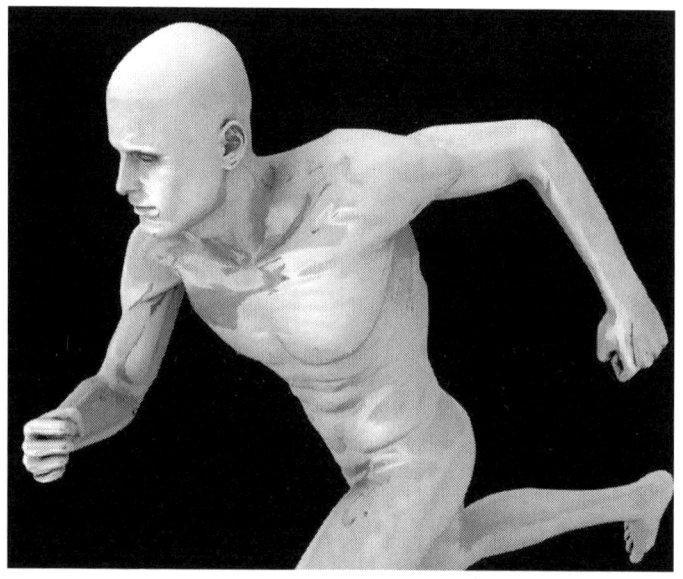

Aim for a purpose-driven life, one where you can see yourself empowered, passionate, enthusiastic, vibrant, vital, and robust. Choose to seek and engage in meaningful and joyous relationships, fulfilling work, and cheerful play. ***Keep your eye on the prize!***

WHAT ON EARTH
AM I HERE FOR?

THE PURPOSE DRIVEN LIFE

Because *health* is your greatest *wealth!*

Don't give to get --
Give to inspire *others*
to give

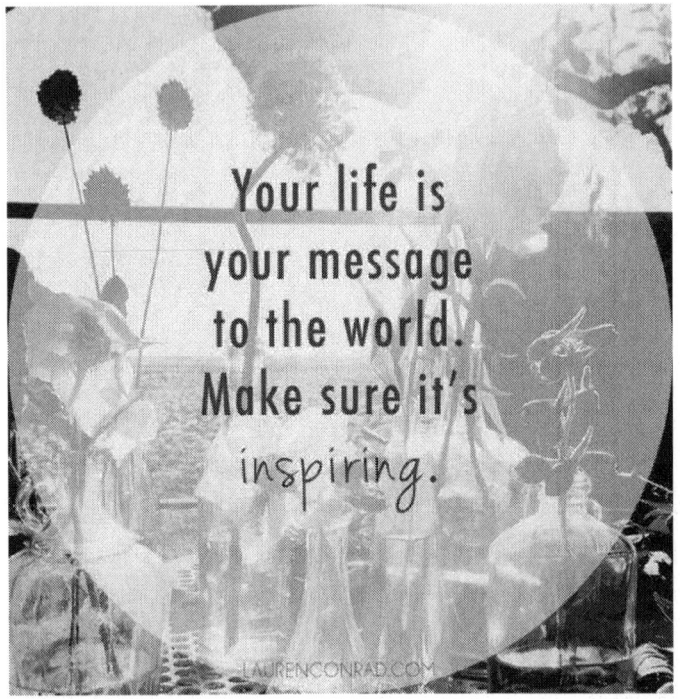

Your life is
your message
to the world.
Make sure it's
inspiring.

LAURENCONRAD.COM

You lose *every* time you don't try.™

Find it *now* – Fix it *right!*

Doing What Works For *YOU!*

Hundreds of "clinics" have recently plunged headlong into the yeast-treatment "business" across the country, despite what might appear to be minimal training and questionable effectiveness of *their* approach. Sure, they heard a lecture or two, maybe even reviewed some YouTube "shorts" or even read a book?

What is frustrating to us is simply this: when a physician with limited experience or marginal understanding advises as 4-week program to "treat your yeast," you might feel somewhat better … but the underlying damage has not been corrected inside your body. And the yeasts continue to thrive.

Some "so-called experts" in "alternative medicine" (or however they brand their practice) can offer you a quickie-treatment for The Yeast Syndrome (you won't know that it's not enough) *then* they can spend dozen of months and dozens of thousands of dollars (*yours!*) struggling to find out how to fix your "remaining" complaints. After all, they can reassure you that they've "already treated your yeast problems," so now they "need to figure out what else" is stealing your comfort, your energy, your vitality.

In many cases we've seen, *hundreds* of pages of test reports have failed to suggest treatment programs to resolve their problems. So ... what really works?

What *we've* found "that works" is to properly treat The Yeast Syndrome – with dietary changes (Meats, Eggs, Vegetables, Yogurt = MEVY), specific nutritional supplements to correct expected chemistry imbalances (and others), changing medications as needed, the whole shebang, the whole "kit and caboodle" – for as long as it takes to produce fundamental changes in a particular patient. All during those months, the program gets *easier* and more *rewarding* as you keep feeling better and better.

That's it. *Not* that hard, right? Doesn't seem that complicated, right?

Then why do "weekend experts" fail to do so? We suspect it's because their training and experience simply means that they haven't returned to the basics, that they haven't studied enough of the complexities, that they don't see "the big picture." How many *years* have many of our patients suffered under their care without really getting "*all* better"?

Now you understand why we deal in *facts* and an increasing body of clinical *experience* ... ours.

This is "not your father's Oldsmobile," to borrow an advertising phrase boasting about all the

Find it *now* – Fix it *right!*

engineering advances in their new model. In many ways, our model sets the standard for evaluating and treating people who unsuspectingly suffer with The Yeast Syndrome. New patients are often surprised that we do "*everything* different" from what they've experienced before.

Everything is different? Think: *concept car!*

While it is unlikely that you'll ever be parking a futuristic Lamborghini in your garage, very likely you *will* be praying for medical treatment that goes a long way to restoring your feeling of health and wellbeing, vitality and enjoyment. When you're suffering through your days and nights, sooner is always better than later.

Why not now?

When life is your choice, failure is not an option.^{SM}
The miracles of healing and repair
proceed with the innate intelligence
given as a priceless blessing to each of us by God,
as a beyond-belief human birthright

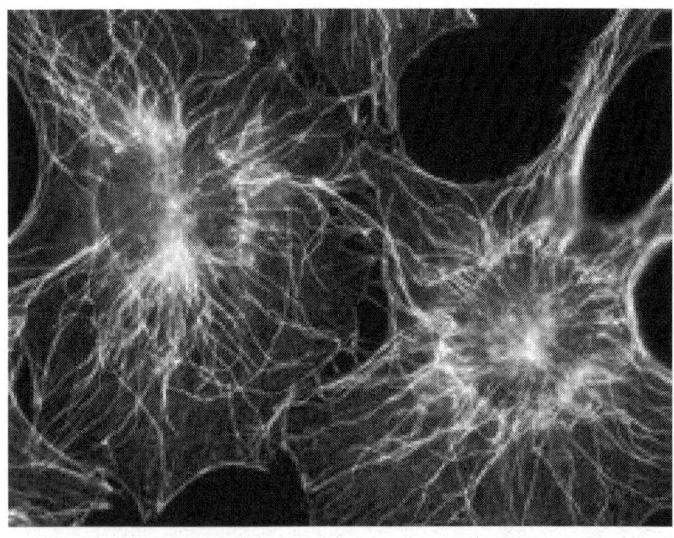

Life … is electrifying!

You lose *every* time you don't try.^{SM}

Find it *now* – Fix it *right!*

Did The Specialists *"Miss It,"* Time And Again?

Yes, they did.

And sadly, **this** story *doesn't* have a happy ending.

Anna Marie came to see me this past fall, accompanied by her husband. A beautiful woman of 34 years old, she had been diagnosed with "lupus" when she was just 19. "Lupus erythematosis" is a "self-against-self" (*autoimmune*) defense system disorder, where your own body mounts an attack against various tissues. Similar to rheumatoid arthritis ("RA"), which attacks your "juicy joints" (hands, knees, others), lupus can attack *anywhere* else, "from the skin on in." Various specialties have different names for lupus-pattern autoimmune attacks seen in different tissues, whether skin or muscle or heart or kidneys or most others, and the presentation can be confused with other diseases, sometimes for years. A positive ANA test ("Anti-Nuclear Antibody") might be a first hint that lupus could be developing and surface in the future.

Anna Marie had "been through all the treatments" – and she was concerned that she was suffering with worsening symptoms despite aggressive drugs, including anti-inflammatories ("NSAIDS," which can cause deadly bleeding), chemotherapy (a common approach), and cortisone ("corticosteroids," also commonly used), and now the specialists had advised "biologic modulators," sometimes called "immune suppressives." (You've seen these constantly advertised on TV as providing wonderful [sometimes *very* expensive] relief ... so long as they don't cause cancer or worsening infections, since they are designed work by changing or even blocking your immune defenses.) As you might expect, she was hesitant to pursue their next step in treatment ... after all, she's a young adult and has hopes for having children in the near future.

What on earth, you might ask, does this have to do with The Yeast Syndrome? Just about ... *everything!* If you have any background studying "yeast," you know that it can create massive damage to your system over time, by leaking out poisons that are absorbed from your gut. These yeast toxins ("Candi-toxins") now number more than 60 – and each one targets specific biochemical reactions in your body metabolism. (Remember that "metabolism" is *everything* you do when you do everything inside.) Yes, that means increasing levels of toxins that can interfere with amino acids and proteins, sugars and starches, oils and fats, minerals, enzymes (the "worker bees" that perform your chemical reactions), energy production pathways (fatigue and weakness!), detoxification pathways, hormones, even nerve transmitters (that means brain function: emotions, brain fog, memory, calculations, muscle coordination, and so on!). Unless, of course, you find proper treatment … **for *yeast!***

So, how hard could *that* be? After all, family practitioners and gynecologists easily treat vaginal yeast infections, dermatologists treat athlete's foot and "jock itch" and various rashes, pediatricians treat "thrush" in the mouth and skin conditions, and so on.

Well, it turns out that treating "*yeast*" is easy – but treating *The Yeast **Syndrome*** is quite a bit more complicated. The problem boils down to this: yeasts that have over-colonized your gut are *not seen* and not readily detected, so no one really thinks of this as a "root cause" of various symptoms or even diseases. Even when yeast doesn't cause an illness, it can dramatically exaggerate your suffering because your biochemistry and defenses simply don't work as well as they should. That, of course, makes your diagnosis and effective treatment much more complicated, because (a lot of) doctors seem to focus on your complaints and prescribe "bandaid drugs" to help you look and feel better.

Why is it difficult for your doctor to discover and treat The Yeast Syndrome? Some people say that it's because the needed treatment program requires them to think in terms of your "physiology" (biochemistry of metabolism) … and that takes time and means recalling concepts from the first and second years of medical school. Tough for some folks, especially when there's a waiting room full of patients ... *still waiting!*

Patients, however, don't make it any easier! What? Stop to think of this: when you have "a problem," you might start with your family doctor (or the physician assistant or nurse practitioner, even a quickie doc-in-box clinic). But if your discomforts persist, you'll finally be referred to – or you'll seek out – a specialist who will focus more on "your area" of concern. For a lupus patient, this could be a rheumatologist or perhaps dermatologist, even others.

I've heard it said that specialists like patients because they bring in their "organ of interest" for evaluation and treatment, then they take it home again rather than leave it lying around the office! What that means is ... you come in with your complaints and you get tests and treatments. If those work, great. If they don't, you'll come back. Time and again. Or you'll get a "second opinion." Maybe time and again.

What about the "problems that just don't go away"? Those are called **chronic diseases**, and modern medicine has a zillion drugs to try to make you more comfortable. And each step along the way *can* result in more complex, more risky, and more expensive care. Such as you might find ... with lupus or rheumatoid arthritis.

Find it *now* – Fix it *right!*

Remember I said that this story doesn't have a happy ending. I've cared for autoimmune illnesses for well over 30 years, usually successfully. (I started graduate studies in immunology in 1968, even considered going on for a Ph.D.) When Anna Marie showed up, her history and tests (she had *many*, from prior doctors) and clinical presentation **clearly** showed her to be suffering with The Yeast Syndrome. (Maybe that's not *all* the treatment she needed – but start reading on page 325 of **THE YEAST SYNDROME** paperback: you'll find 10 pages of autoimmune disorders! You have to search for "autoimmune" in the ebook version.) I spent an hour explaining her condition and treatment program and answering questions from her and her husband. We gave her a CD recording of our initial office visit, including explanations of the many earlier tests she had undergone.

Days later, when my nurse called to be sure we had explained her situation well enough. She said she felt overwhelmed, that she felt like she would have to quit her job in order to start the program. (All *that* means is she was to follow specific eating guidelines and take specific nutritional supplements.) Her follow-up statement was shocking: "My husband and I have decided that I should wait until I really feel able to do it."

Instead, she'll do more of what didn't help her before. Sad but true.

Because *health* is your greatest *wealth!*

If you're "*staying sick*" with your modern medical care, consider this: Please ***don't complain*** about the *results that you're **not getting*** from the *program that you're **not doing***, especially if that might be "the one" that **could** help you feel much better.

The time is *now* to find ways to improve your health – and especially to avoid future illnesses and lingering discomforts that can steal your life and your happiness. Some people wait too late … then they never "feel well enough" to do what is needed for an effective healing program … and they choose instead more drugs, more surgery … often the same treatments that didn't help them before.

> "If you have a heartbeat, there's still time for your dreams."

You lose *every* time you don't try.^{SM}

Find it ***now*** – Fix it ***right!***

"I've Never *Had* A Yeast Infection"

Of course not! Richard is a **guy**, and we all know that only **gals** "get yeast," right?

So … humor me – let's see just how many specialists were needed to treat Richard's problems over his lifetime – and especially now that he's in his early 70s.

His mother said he was "a gassy baby – and cried a lot." The doctor said he "had thrush" (a yeast infection in the mouth, more often seen in babies). Back in "the old days," medical science had far fewer options for *any* treatments than they we have now. (In many ways, "older" approaches were overall safer and better than today's.) He doesn't really know but sort of recalls that Mom talked about using lem*on* juice, which made him cry. ***Pediatrician***. That was his first specialist; they "started" in 1930. The doctor never related his thrush to the diaper rash he suffered early on – for which he advised corn starch. Entirely the ***wrong*** thing to do.

[Just for kicks, the years when "new" medical specialties arose or when some of the drugs became available are included here. Why? So you can see that *much* of the medical practice we experience has ***come about very recently***. Makes you wonder why physicians often have such a resistance to your seeking alternatives now available in the field of "integrative medicine" – an approach that combines traditional training and treatments with effective ones from the past and newer ones from emerging scientific discoveries. Indeed, as physicians, I think we should be all about discovering *what works best for our patients*. What do you think?]

As a kid, Rick had a funky rash that came and went, here and there. His *GP* (General Practitioner, the "original" doctors) didn't really have an answer but advised olive oil applications. Didn't help much but didn't hurt him either. Cortisone didn't come along until 1949 – and that can *worsen* the cause of many rashes but often provides brief comfort. Formal recognition of "**Family Practice**" docs came along in 1947 (or 1971), finally blossoming to become one of the largest physician organizations. Now, of course, they're "just" your "*PCP*" (primary care "provider"), unless instead you see their physician assistant (PA, 1960s-70s) or nurse practitioner (NP, 1960s-70s).

As a teenager, Rick suffered with athlete's foot and "jock itch." And, of course, acne. For which he was prescribed cortisone creams along with oral and topical antibiotics. Sure, these seemed to help … but not exactly the best treatments we have now, even when not prescribed by many physicians. The *Dermatologist* offered these treatments. These specialists have been around since 1933.

Find it *now* – Fix it *right!*

Rick grew into young adulthood with few problems, even joined the Navy. (Founded in 1775, in case you were wondering; check these other historical years!) Complaining of feeling tired as years past, he saw a medical ***corpsman*** (1814, but really earlier for wartime), who scheduled a visit with the **Navy base physician** (a general medical officer, often like a GP, 1871), who happened to be an ***Internal Medicine*** specialist (1936). Diagnosed with hypothyroidism, Rick started on a prescription for natural thyroid medication (1891, Armour Thyroid), which helped a lot.

But his woes were not over. Rick started complaining of "heartburn," and the corpsman referred him to the base specialist. Yep, ***Gastroenterologist*** (1932). A barium "upper GI x-ray series" (1910) by a ***Radiologist*** (1935) was followed by visual inspection of his esophagus swallowing tube and stomach with the flexible gastroscope (1958). Rick was advised to follow an "ulcer diet" and take cimetidine (1977, Tagamet), an acid-secretion blocker. But he continued to suffer belly pains (and burping) every time he stopped the drug. The specialist shifted him to sucralfate (1981, Carafate), which covers raw, ulcerated areas rather like a scab covers open skin wounds but has aluminum. Rick finally "got better" but never felt fully well.

In later years, dandruff started to be a constant concern. Again, he saw a **_Dermatologist_**, who prescribed cortisone shampoo, creams, and lotions (1950s) for his scalp. What a frustrating and almost daily problem for Rick! Incidentally, these are usually the **_wrong_** treatment, even though still widely used, partly because they can encourage the growth of more yeast.

Yes, his **_Dentist_** (1859 – what did they really do earlier?) got into the action too. Since Rick had advanced periodontal gum disease, he was referred to a **_Periodontist_** (1914) … who suggested gum surgery and antibiotics … and a thorough "cleaning" every 3 months. The specialist also noted white patches, called leukoplakia, on his mouth tissues and advised surgical removal to reduce chances of "malignant transformation" (cancer changes), since no treatment is uniformly successful in their hands.

At one point, his new **Family Practitioner** insisted on changing his thyroid medication to straight thyroxine (1930s, Synthroid) – but the effects weren't as desired and Rick ended up seeing an **_Endocrinologist_** (1991). That didn't work out so well and he finally found an old-time **_GP_** who restarted Armour® thyroid once again.

As he grew older, Rick was suffering with more problems as well. By this time, his joints and muscles were aching and painful, especially in the

Find it **_now_** – Fix it **_right!_**

mornings, especially after extra activities such as working in the yard or walking more with travels. Tests by his **"PCP"** showed early rheumatoid arthritis changes, for which chemotherapy was considered by the *Rheumatologist* (1932) he saw. Rick chose instead to try over-the-counter aspirin and acetaminophen, even ibuprofen (Motrin/Advil, 1984 – prescription starting in 1974). Happily, this NSAID (non-steroidal anti-inflammatory drug – several are available now, mostly by prescription) sure made his joints and muscles feel better … but *un*happily his stomach pains grew worse. Back to the *Gastroenterologist*. Now Rick needed aggressive treatment for a peptic ulcer related to the daily use of ibuprofen; this time a "protein pump inhibitor" was advised (Prilosec, 1989). Antacids such as aluminum/magnesium hydroxide (Maalox, 1949) helped provide more comfort … but are loaded with toxic aluminum.

Every time he tried to stop the stomach medications, his discomforts returned – because treatment is much more involved than just "blockers." So Rick continued various over-the-counter acid-interrupting drugs and antacids off and on for years – not realizing that they reduce the "acid-bath" that helps protect from infections coming in with foods, reduce processing of needed proteins (meats and such), and reduce absorption of various minerals. Eventually Rick was found to have osteopenia (on the way to osteoporosis, softening bones) and his *Internist* (1936) prescribed a bisphosphonate (Fosamax, 1995) to reduce bone fracture risk. Unfortunately, *that* drug caused more inflammation of his swallowing tube (esophagus) and stomach, leading to more evaluation (scopes!) and treatment by the *Gastroenterologist*. Not to mention an increased risk for "dead jaw syndrome" (osteonecrosis), impossible to reverse.

Enough specialists for you? But wait – there's more. Rick saw a *Podiatrist* (1895) for severe fungal infections of his toenails (onychomycosis), and surgical removal of the great toe toenails was very painful but produced *some* improvement. Still, the other toenails had problems – and the prescribed anti-fungal medication (1996, terbinifine, Lamisil) simply wasn't working.

In his later 60s, his PSA (prostate blood test) rose to abnormal levels. The *Urologist* (1902) biopsied and found prostate cancer cells. The proposed treatments – prostate removal or chemotherapy or hormone therapy – just didn't sound appealing. That's when aggressive, high-dose treatment for The Yeast Syndrome was started – with stunning results. [Have your friends look at this interesting article on the internet: https://www.cancertutor.com/currentstudy/ – just be cautious, don't experiment with all sorts of "treatments" and diets that you read about on the internet.]

Find it *now* – Fix it *right!*

What about his many other physical problems – some of which aren't even recounted here: headaches, recurrent sinus and ear infections and bronchitis, one episode of pneumonia, even "brain fog" and bothersome forgetfulness, to name just a few. A pretty average guy, overall.

Guess what – virtually **ALL** of the illness episodes recounted here can trace their *roots* … or at least their *worsening and persistence* of discomforts … to The Yeast Syndrome.

So … Rick "**never** had a yeast infection," *is that so?* But he had **many** problems "associated with" yeast – and none of the specialists or general doctors could ever figure out the cause of his many symptoms … and none ever treated it appropriately. Sadly, this is much more common that you would *ever* expect.

Oh, yes – Rick is feeling *much better* now, due to a comprehensive "integrative" program not only for The Yeast Syndrome but also for the many other challenging "domino diseases" that have befallen him over the past 70-plus years.

You lose *every* time you don't try.^{sm}

Here's a fun exercise to help convince you that seeing yourself getting healthy with The Yeast Syndrome is something where *you've hardly ever had a chance* … until now!

Ask your friends or family members the following questions:

1. Has your doctor explained why you're taking any medications?

2. Has your doctor told you when you'll be able to stop your medications?

3. Has your doctor told you that you're "going to get *all better*" *or* that you're likely to continue to *suffer* with problems in the future?

So … how can you ever expect to "get better," for real?

Life is much more than *hopeful* "betting" on red or black or green or odds or evens at the roulette table!

You lose *every* time you don't try.℠

Find it *now* – Fix it *right!*

Who Wants To Live To Be 100?

Only folks who are *currently 99* and *feeling okay!*

One thing is certain: people who don't feel well, especially when every year brings more discomforts and drugs into their life … they become resigned to dying early because suffering each day simply isn't worth it.

While many claim they "want to live forever" – or maybe 100 or whatever … what you really mean is that you want to live as long as you remain both …

<u>C</u>**omfortable**
and
<u>C</u>**apable**.

For too many years, we've witnessed our seniors debilitated with aches and pains, where drugs provide little relief, longing for rest of any kind. Successful treatment when The Yeast Syndrome is creating daily misery can, at the very least, keep *you* living independently and free of distress or discomfort … for a long time to come.

"The best doctor in the world is the veterinarian. He can't ask his patients what is the matter – he's got to just know." American actor, writer, and humorist "Will" Rogers might be onto something there … but I haven't yet found a vet who will take care of *me!* So I have had to place my faith in …

THE SECRET FORMULA:

$$2\,C + 2\,C = A+$$

Honestly, there are no secrets. Mastering success with your doctoring is quite simple when you take personal responsibility for your health care. *Your* responsibilities are summed up as " **2 C** ":

Curious patient, ***Compliant*** patient.

Plus the *doctors* you seek have obligations that also add up to " **2 C** ":

Competent doctor, ***Communicating*** doctor.

The result is an **A+** in your life!

As a caring and curious physician, I was blessed that I "stumbled" early in my career to discover the immense power of natural healing. I have been driven to blaze a trail for patients *and* their doctors, leading to distant horizons of exceptional results with both *medical* **and** *health* care.

The secrets to "doctoring" are easy: study intently the emerging sciences, seek many details from your patients, ask probing questions and then listen intently, perform competent hands-on exams, and order and understand advanced tests that unlock

Find it *now* – Fix it ***right!***

the *secret* causes of inflammation, toxicities, deficiencies, and failing functions ... so that they can finally be corrected rather than merely bandaged without ever realizing what was happening.

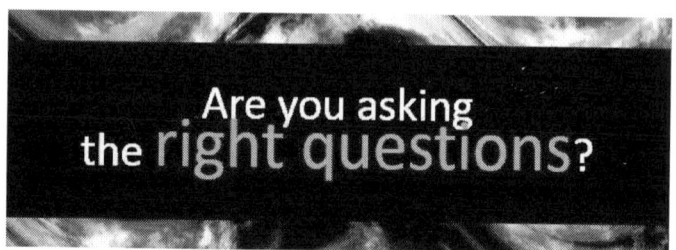

You lose *every* time you don't try.™

Because *health* is your greatest *wealth!*

Quick Questions

What tests have you had that never seemed to make sense to you?

What "diagnoses" have you been offered that never seemed to make sense to you?

Which family members or friends need to hear about these ideas now?

Other answers I am looking to find today:

You lose *every* time you don't try.^{SM}

Find it *now* – Fix it *right!*

"I Don't Enjoy 'The Go' Anymore!"

How many times have you heard from a doctor that *your* bowel habits are "okay," people just vary a great deal but most everyone is normal? Your complaints about diarrhea or constipation (or *both!*) seem to fall on deaf ears – or you get casual advice, perhaps a prescription you don't want and maybe can't afford.

The same might be said to you when you complain of belly bloating, belching or passing gas, even heartburn or rolling belly pains. Shouldn't your treatment be much more than reassurance or "gut drugs"?

Too many times, on a later return visit, you could get told that you just need to "learn to live with it." You *already* know how to live **with** it – you want to live **without** it!

Dozens of millions of Americans suffer with IBS or "irritable bowel syndrome." This frustrating and painful condition is one where bowel movements can swing unpredictably from constipation to diarrhea and back. Some people are so miserable that they become prisoners in their own home, unwilling to risk embarrassment or discomfort when out and about. Plane trips might be totally out of the question, even long drives as well. Will you miss joining your family and friends for years to come?

Will you miss seeing your children and grandchildren grow older, getting together only when *they* come to town?

Before we get too far, let's be sure that your symptoms are not confused with "***inflammatory*** bowel syndrome." You might have seen TV advertisements for fancy new drugs (with ominous side effects) for these gut diseases, often referred to as Crohn's or ulcerative colitis. Rest assured that competent medical diagnosis is essential but that effective treatment is available – usually without cortisone or chemotherapy or other recent medications – and the principles of healing are very similar to that with IBS.

Sadly, many specialists haven't a clue, they simply don't know the cause of your problem. And that, of course, is why they reassure you that they've done *all* that can be done – and usher you out of the office. Check Dr. Google, but don't hold your breath: "No one knows the cause ..." Further, no one has been able to confirm a specific cause for inflammatory bowel syndromes either.

Simple question: why does a doctor who doesn't have a clue about how to treat you assume that no ***other*** doctor can know the cause either? As great as you think your doctor "is," what if he or she simply doesn't know about advanced treatments ... or even "alternative" approaches that might provide the chance for you to become healed and free of these

Find it ***now*** – Fix it ***right!***

discomforts? Could turning to a doctor with suitable expertise return you to more enjoyment and optimism every day for the rest of your life?

You're reading this article to learn how yeast might create or contribute to your problems. But my aim is to have your discomforts *completely* corrected, so let's start with some basics. Food selection is critical: rather than soft or mushy foods, choose a variety of crunchy vegetables, in a rainbow of colors, each day. Chew each bite 30 or more times, to break down the consistency and allow digestive enzymes to mix easily, starting with those in your mouth. Every day, drink enough water – you've heard that advice before!

Your stomach churns the foods to allow hydrochloric acid to digest your proteins and prepare your minerals for absorption. A surprising (and increasing) percentage of adults produce less stomach acid after the age of 35, so many problems can start here. Your pancreas and gallbladder (or liver, if your gallbladder was removed) provide more enzymes and bile salts, to digest and absorb starches and sugars, fats and proteins, as the slurry flows through your small intestine.

Your colon (large intestine) removes precious water and minerals, so your stool is concentrated and easy to pass. Most of the bacteria (good and bad), yeasts, and parasites take up residence here – the collection is called your "microbiome" (mī-krō-

BUY'-ōhm). Everyone has a different pattern, based upon *all* your past experiences, including nursing as an infant, food and supplement selections, antibiotics and cortisone, illnesses, and so on. Even your own pattern will change over time. However, once various episodes "bump" out of line the balance in your gut flora (another name for the collection), some changes might never return to normal.

Now for the good stuff: *everyone* grows yeasts inside, particularly in the colon. The common species found in humans is *Candida albicans* (CAN'-dih-duh al-bih-cans) . Others can grow as well, but the key feature is that your bacteria, digestive juices, and antibodies generally keep these yeasts "in check." They don't bother you … and you don't bother them. Most experiences that alter your microbiome (especially antibiotics and corticosteroids) *favor* the overgrowth of yeasts. This and other distorted patterns can lead to cramping and bloating, belching and passing gas, altered stool form and consistency, diarrhea and constipation. Of course you *don't* "enjoy 'The Go'" anymore!

When yeasts grow inside your gut, they put out specific waste products called "Candi-toxins" (CAN''-dih-tocks'-inz). Your colon *absorbs these as well*, along with water and minerals, and they are *targeted* to disable specific biochemical reactions inside your tissues. As your functions fail, the yeast is gradually making a Happy Meal® out of you: you become sick with a variety of problems, you might

Find it *now* – Fix it ***right!***

even jump on the medical merry-go-round seeking specialists who can truly treat your many concerns. The sicker you get, the more antibiotics and other drugs you get, the more the yeasts grow in you gut, the more toxins are absorbed to bang on your systems, the cycle worsens, and you fail further until you finally die.

Along the way, your gut function can become distorted: when diarrhea and constipation patterns set in, we often call that "irritable bowel syndrome." So … the treatment you *need* becomes easy to see when you *know the cause!*

Where does all this leave *you?* Some people suffer for years. Even decades. Obviously there's no one simple answer, and certainly a brief book cannot make *you* well. My goal is to motivate you to search further for "the right answer" that heals *your* problem – and to offer some comfort measures you can choose now as part of a program to solve your distress.

You might not realize how important it is for you to have a more normal bowel program. Chronic constipation has been associated with *colon* cancer, and that seems reasonable. But consider this startling fact: having less than 1 bowel movement a week (once every 8 *or more* days) was found 40 years ago to relate to the highest risk for ***breast*** cancer; women having more than 1 a day (8 or more movements in a week) showed the lowest risk. Bowel blockages causing constipation can be due to colon or other cancers, infections, certain female problems (like endometriosis), even frustrating internal changes after a belly operation. *Caution*: long-standing problems that fail to improve *can be* life-threatening: they need to be properly diagnosed and closely followed by your physician until better. Persistent diarrhea can be similarly worrisome, so take prudent steps to secure the care you need for your better future health.

The list of body changes is impressive, affecting *all* the systems of your body, especially symptoms you would *never* relate to gut problems. Many other discomforts – rashes, frequent sore throats or ear or sinus infections, memory changes, fatigue, brain fog, body aches and pains, the list goes on and on – might get a whole lot better with treatment for The Yeast Syndrome. Many people who have been on the medical merry-go-round for years, spinning from doctor-to-specialist-and-back, stacking on drugs and operations, can suddenly find relief due to treatment for the **un**suspected problem that could be the cause of so *many* of their illness issues.

But *your* answer (even "answers," since problems often worsen like falling dominos) should be right around the next corner. So … I insist that you search until you see a doctor who *can **find it now** and **fix it right!***sm

Sadly, *your* doctor *just said* … "I don't believe in all that silliness." Or "quackery." Or whatever. Time for you to ask for referral to a *better doctor*, here defined as someone willing to work *with* you – not against you! – to do whatever it takes to finally resolve *your* suffering. Being insistent might be embarrassing at first … but are you willing to suffer in silence for a few more **years** just because *your* doctor is *down on* what he or she is not *up on*?

So what is The Yeast Syndrome and how should you treat it? Here's key concept: it is ***not*** a simple "yeast infection." A syndrome is a collection of signs (obvious changes) and symptoms (discomforts) that can be found together, related to a common *cause*. For most people, the common yeast in your gut has taken over, silently and secretly growing out of control due to antibiotics, cortisone and other hormones, dietary excesses of sugars and starches, unknown nutritional deficiencies, even unexpected toxic exposures to chemicals or heavy metals (mercury in your fillings would be a good example).

The Yeast Syndrome isn't a simple problem, and treatment can take several months, even a couple of years. Yeasts are sinister and terribly smart, so they trick and disable your immune defense system. Meanwhile, they continue to saturate your system with poisons that damage your biochemical processes. You might not realize it, but members of the "fungus kingdom" (yeasts, fungus, molds, and mildew) are designed to recycle *all* members of the "plant kingdom" and the "animal kingdom." (We're part of the last one.) Nothing personal, just business.

Perhaps even more ominous is our finding that some patients are harboring a Deep Blood Fungus – related to but different from The Yeast Syndrome – and they require much more complex treatment programs. These people can suffer with more than just a serious *inflammatory* bowel syndrome but also various cancers, blood cancers, severe skin conditions, sudden kidney failure, worsening diabetes, MS (multiple sclerosis), ALS (Lou Gehrig's disease), RA (rheumatoid arthritis), SLE (lupus), vague immune defense system disorders, and others. The laboratory performing our tests has used their genetic sequencing test to confirm deep fungus evidence in the plaque blocking heart arteries (our *leading* cause of death) and in other body organs.

Let's review practical steps that might help you resolve suffering with simpler gut problems, even heartburn and hemorrhoids! *Aging* is a *disease* happening one day at a time. Suffering with The Yeast Syndrome can make your aging go faster, stealing your vitality and enthusiasm. *And* your hope for relief in the future. You *can* find treatment that really helps, no matter how many years you have suffered and no matter how far you fear your problems have worsened. Keep your eye on the prize!

Find it *now* – Fix it *right!*

Better digestion literally starts with your food selection and preparation. And, yes, organic vegetables are worth the expense, they can "feed" your cells better than you might imagine. Same with organically-grown meats … and eggs … and yogurt. *Over*cooking your foods is crazy, so don't! Steaming vegetables is wonderful for preserving flavor and nutritional factors and quick enough to do. Even combing foods such as carbohydrates (sugars and starches) with proteins (such as meats) at the same time can affect your body chemistry negatively. "Eating out" usually means "fast foods," not good. Loads of ideas are presented in the Celebration of Healthy Eating, especially "Phase I" foods, in my 1986 Bantam Books best-seller, **THE YEAST SYNDROME**. (This is years ahead of the *paleo* …)

Here's a fun exercise: go to the TV dinners aisle at your local supermarket, take along a pen and paper, write down every different meat and vegetable available in those packages. You'll be startled at the limited food selection – and the lack of fiber, also known as "roughage," essential for good bowel movements. I have long emphasized "the Crunchy-C's" … celery, carrots, cauliflower, broccoli, Brussels sprouts, and so on. Yogurt or sour cream, mixed with your choice of spices, makes a great dip for an awesome snack *with* these vegetables.

Next, take enough time to eat – avoid eating on the run or in too short a time, hurrying to get on with the rest of your day. Pleasant conversation

Because *health* is your greatest *wealth!*

helps digestion as well. Chew each bite at least 30 times and avoid the temptation to swallow with a slug of water. Incidentally, drinking several glasses of water daily is a great habit, one that most folks ignore! Here's a trick if heartburn troubles you – instead of drugs that can interrupt vital functions, mix aloe vera (juice or gel) with an equal volume of papaya (juice or gel): sip straight or pour over ice, keep in the refrigerator or in a thermos at work or in your car.

Your capability to produce sufficient stomach acids, pancreatic enzymes, and bile salts critical for digestion can decline over the decades of adulthood. Integrative medicine specialists have simple tests to evaluate your situation and have precise supplements to correct deficiencies. You might be startled at how simple this approach could be. These items could be the most important steps to begin now *and continue for years*, to resolve your irritable bowel symptoms and many other gut complaints.

You might have learned a bit about your microbiome – the collection of bacteria, yeasts, parasites, viruses mostly found in your colon (large intestine). Two strategies are important to rebalance your gut: *pre*biotics and *pro*biotics. Prebiotics are substances that encourage the growth or activity of microorganisms inside. In general, prebiotics are natural undigestible plant fibers in foods, best when eaten raw not cooked. One easily available substance is inulin, easily available in "gummies" over-the-

Find it *now* – Fix it *right!*

counter at your pharmacy. Probiotics are various strains of gut bacteria – they vary widely in many preparations, some refrigerated, some not – taken to encourage replacement of a more normal microbiome pattern. Every time you take antibiotics or cortisone, you might need many months to supplement with adequate probiotics.

What about "fiber"? That burning question has been the topic of TV advertisements for years. Health food stores have long offered psyllium seed husks – as tasty as ground-up cardboard! Any powdered product you use can be mixed with drinks or powdered on foods, to improve palatability. Be careful not to add too much too quickly to your daily intake, but know that more fiber is generally associated with better health as you grow older. Some studies show positive effects on your circulation as well, such as reducing heart disease risks. Chewing high-fiber foods helps digestion as well as creating a proper sense of fullness, to reduce overeating.

Let's get down-n-dirty about yeast. At the very start – literally! – yeast can overgrow in your mouth, on your tongue (check for a whitish or yellowish coating) or your gums (often reddened, swollen, tender). Overgrowth here easily "seeds" your swallowing tube and the rest of your gut and *complete* treatment is required! Gum disorders – periodontitis (pair'-ē-ō-dawn-tight'-iss) – can be particularly ominous, since these changes might

Because *health* is your greatest *wealth!*

appear likely to encourage Deep Blood Fungus infections to enter, take root, and grow in your blood and organs. [More on this in later books, including how to dramatically improve the health of your gums and teeth without surgery.]

As yeast colonize your colon (large intestine) and blossom more and more out of control, they leak out various toxins that your body absorbs along with water and minerals. These poisons (Candi-toxins) target vital biochemical reactions inside your cells, gradually stealing your health and comfort. The nutritional support program you need for recovery from The Yeast Syndrome is based on repairing and restoring these damaged functions in organs throughout your body, from brain to "bottom" and on down.

One of the most significant interruptions is with the final conversion of essential fatty acids (like EPA, as in fish oil) to the active forms used by your body. Does this sound "too technical"? Well, how's this: supplementing with enough high-quality, very carefully processed omega-3 oils over a long enough time … can help many organs to repair and can restore much more normal gut function – that means your bowel movements!

So-called irritable bowel syndrome often results from damage to your essential fatty acids, thanks to yeast toxins. You're not short of drugs, you're not suffering with a dangerous illness, instead

Find it *now* – Fix it *right!*

you have nutritional deficiencies thanks to being poisoned by abnormal yeast growth in your "toxic waste dump," your colon. How easy is *that?*

The rest of your treatment program for The Yeast Syndrome aims at reversing the damage done to your various organs and functions: limiting sugars and starches, limiting allergy-provoking foods, supplementing with Vitamin B_6, magnesium, Vitamin C, and others. All of these are well described in my Bantam book, along with a variety of recipes and other hints to make your life easier and better. Always remember that *complete* treatment involves appropriate prescription medications, continued long enough, in order to restore your immune defense system to full competence and your body systems to full capability.

As you might imagine, diarrhea and/or constipation can be even more uncomfortable if they provoke or even create hemorrhoids. An old fashioned approach is to use moist witch hazel pads or tissues after wiping, to assist cleaning and comfort. After that, you might consider using the ointment or cream version of Preparation H *with Biodyne*, available from amazon.ca (Canada) because the U.S. FDA insisted that these active components be removed. We have another useful trick: apply a soothing and protective skin cream that encourages rapid healing, as it contains Vitamins E, D, A, and B_5. If your "bottom" is really uncomfortable, consider soaking in a warm shallow sitz bath to

which you've added a packet or two of Domeboro®
astringent … you can also use as a wet compress if
better than soaking.

Hemorrhoids are frustrating to so many
people, but sometimes they can be downright
dangerous. Be sure to see a gastroenterologist or
colorectal surgeon if you see unexpected blood in
your stools, persistent blood (even if just on the
tissue), worrisome bleeding, or anal pains. Most of
the cancers in the colon happen close to "the end"
and are better and more easily treated when
discovered early, so be prudent and protect your
health.

One last point worth mentioning: your skilled
and experienced integrative physician has available a
number of tests that can pinpoint areas needing
assistance or repair all along your gut. Serious
diseases can arise and threaten your wellbeing, so be
sure that your problems correct quickly and
completely, so that you really *can* "enjoy 'The Go.'"
Always insist on proper treatment from a competent
professional with sufficient training and expertise.
You *can* find treatment that really helps, no matter
how many years you have suffered and no matter
how far you fear your problems have worsened.

Keep your eye on the prize, better health
literally could be around the corner!

You lose *every* time you don't try.^{SM}

Find it *now* – Fix it *right!*

Just Waiting On *You*

We're standing by, ready and willing and able, whenever you choose to reach for a brighter, more rewarding future.

More than that, we see clearly that *our* job is "Just **Waiting On** You" – *we* know that *we're* here to **meet your needs**. Not to do tests or push pills or stick needles. Not to rush you in and out because dozens of others are piling into our lobby. Not to brush off your questions as we're leaving the room. Not to ignore your phone calls or faxes or emails when you really need answers.

YOU are here for results … not for the experience. *We* are here to be **waiting on** you, just like the capable waiters that serve your every need and make your dining experience so enjoyable in the finest restaurants.

Awesome Staff Of Life Celebrating Health

We're thrilled that he's the boss, developing incredibly successful diagnosis and treatment programs that we almost always see are helping our desperate and frustrated patients to get out of their pain and get on with their life … *regardless* of the problems with which they have been suffering.

Because *health* is your greatest *wealth!*   105

And like all great leaders, he absolutely relies on a well trained, enthusiastic, and reassuring staff to help meet the needs of those we serve.

Some folks are impressed with the "trappings" of impressive downtown buildings, high-rise elevators, expensive décor, fancy equipment, and the hushed formality of many medical offices.

What Dr. T values is … *us!* We show up each day bright-eyed and committed to make an amazing (occasionally unbelievable) difference, meeting the personal needs in *each* patient's life. Many of those who depend on us come from a long distance – and they cherish our single focus on meeting their needs. Our patients give meaning and purpose to our lives.

Our Senior Staff

Cathy – 27 years	Rena – 27 years
Michelle – 13 years	Lucrecia – 6 years

Our Rookies In the Dugout

Brooke – 3 years	Ebony – 1 year

So the only question for us to ask right now is …

"What may we do for *you* today?"

You lose *every* time you don't try.^{SM}

Find it *now* – Fix it *right!*

Treating The Yeast Syndrome:
Boring!

If you don't believe it, just ask Jennifer.

That was her comment after staying on Phase I of "the eating program" (*she* called it a "*diet*") for 4 months.[5] *But* … she did lose unwanted pounds and started slimming down to fit her clothes. And she gained dramatically in energy, comfort, and restful sleep. More on her in just a minute.

As an acknowledged specialist treating The Yeast Syndrome, I have heard "boring" as a comment from newbie physicians who have heard a lecture on "treating yeast." They have concluded that "you just tell them to avoid sugars and starches and give them a prescription for a yeast-killer for a few weeks." If *that* were all there is to it, sure, that *would* be boring.

The key feature for The Yeast *Syndrome* is that treating the "infection" is merely a first step in repairing the damage that results from the yeast toxins and other biochemical changes – *those* features are "*the syndrome*." An **infection** is the invasion of a body tissue by pathological organisms (bacteria, viruses, fungi/yeasts, parasites) that multiply and create tissue damage, leading to disease. A

---

[5] Phase I of the Celebration of Healthy Eating documented in detail in **The Yeast Syndrome** book, starting with **MEVY**: **M**eats, **E**ggs, **V**egetables, and **Y**ogurt – altered as needed for each particular patient. (Years before *paleo* …) Because *health* is your greatest *wealth!*

syndrome, however, is a particular *group* of symptoms (distressing complaints) or signs (measurable problems, such as fever or swelling) that characterize a disorder. "Irritable bowel syndrome" (IBS) is an example, as is "premenstrual syndrome" (PMS). One of the more recent ones is "Metabolic Syndrome" (originally designated "Syndrome X" because of the confusing pattern), where changes in your sugar handling can lead to weight gain, serious blood vessel problems, and high blood pressure, even later heart disease, strokes, and diabetes.[6]

But here is where the story gets "tricky." There is no "one" collection of symptoms that is characteristic of The Yeast *Syndrome*. So the very **same** diagnosis (of "yeast") can be offered to ten patients in a row, each presenting with dramatically different complaints. In past centuries, syphilis was called "The Great Pretender," since its symptoms can look like many other diseases. The next to gain that title was tuberculosis (TB), again because it can mimic disorders in virtually any organ system. Addison's disease (severe dysfunction of the adrenal stress glands) was recognized as ... not being easily recognizable. Proper treatment of AIDS (Acquired

---

[6] I was privileged to meet endocrinologist Gerald M. ("Jerry") Reaven, M.D., in 1968, while he was a young professor and I was a pre-med student at Stanford, when he was beginning his research leading to discovering "Metabolic Syndrome," a prelude to diabetes. His studies on insulin resistance confirmed that excess sugars and starches contribute to *many* of our degenerative diseases. Could one of the mechanisms be that they encourage development and worsening of The Yeast Syndrome ... and even devastating Deep Blood Fungus? More research could give powerful answers for diagnosis and treatment.

Find it *now* – Fix it ***right!***

Immune Deficiency Syndrome), often associated
with HIV (Human Immunodeficiency Virus), has
required physicians to understand changes in many
different systems. So-called "Chronic Fatigue
Syndrome" (also "fibromyalgia") can be puzzling as
well. In recent decades, special tests have helped
physicians to see such problems at an earlier time.
The Yeast Syndrome, however, "takes the cake" (and
no, you shouldn't!) in this modern era as being able
to masquerade as any number of diseases (illnesses)
or disorders (disturbed function) in *each and every*
organ system, where the underlying cause is very
often missed by conventional doctors.

You're getting a glimpse as to why
diagnosing The Yeast Syndrome is so complicated:
your doctor has to keep an eye out for other (also
serious) causes for your exact same symptoms.
Sadly, there's **no "good test"** to show that you *do* –
or that you *don't* – suffer with The Yeast Syndrome.
The clinical art is in taking the time to review your
history, to carefully listen to your current complaints,
to examine your body, and to order needed tests to
show that you *don't* have other explanations for your
problems. Here's a glitch: being thorough takes time
and some doctors simply *can't*, *don't*, or *won't* take
the time with you – and *that's* making the assumption
that the he or she actually understands and *is looking
for* The Yeast Syndrome. (You won't "fix" what you
don't treat, you won't treat what you don't find, you
won't find what you're not looking for – and you
won't look for what you don't know about!)

Because *health* is your greatest *wealth!*

Jennifer is a classic patient: in her mid-20s, she was simply too tired to enjoy life, almost daily headaches hampered her comfort, belly bloating was a constant companion, her sinuses were congested and her ears rang constantly. Not to mention her sugar cravings – and the pounds she had piled on unexpectedly. She was too tired to exercise, which she used to enjoy. More troubling, though, was the puzzling rash that started on her right shin and finally had spread to her belly, her arms, her upper legs, and her back ... and all that the dermatologist offered was cortisone (steroids) or antihistamines. Jennifer's cycles had been irregular since first starting, and sometimes she went 3 months between periods (don't forget the painful PMS). Another doctor's hormones over 6 years never balanced her system and birth control pills just worsened her moods and her weight.

Fast-forward 4 months. Jennifer is boasting that her rash is gone, her fatigue is better, her headaches are gone, her ears no longer ring, her memory is better, she's down one pants size, and her facial blemishes are gone. Her hormones are normalizing and her belly is just fine. In her words, "I'm doing great. I stay up late, I get up early, *I'm living life!*"

So ... what was "boring" in the midst of all these wonderful changes? The Phase I program for eating, of course! What was Jennifer's reward for following her personalized treatment guidelines so well? She gets to gradually add foods from Phase II, for variety and enjoyment. We're busy "fixing" her thyroid, her gallbladder, her pancreas dysfunction, her "leaky gut" and more – all the things that The Yeast Syndrome can create as problems, just like falling dominos.

So here's where it really gets exciting – *not at all boring!* Everyone knows about "yeast infections" causing distressing reddened skin ("jock itch" or under-the-breasts irritation), even a troublesome vaginal discharge and so on. But what many people (and even doctors) don't realize is that The Yeast *Syndrome* can, *itself*, *cause* *other* *syndromes!* Such as … irritable bowel syndrome, PMS, adrenal exhaustion syndrome, and on and on and on. Not too much fun for the patients suffering – but really fascinating for specialists like me.

The greatest problem with treating The Yeast *Syndrome* is that inexperienced or well-meaning but uninformed doctors assume that "treating" for just a few weeks is sufficient. Then you can spend dozens of thousands of dollars and dozens of months with their well-meaning but misguided efforts "trying to figure out what *else* is wrong," since (as they mistakenly explain) you've "already been treated for yeast." Nope. Wrong, wrong, wrong!

Isn't it time for you (or someone in your family?) to finally fix health problems (serious and minor, but *always* troubling) caused by the newest "The Great Pretender"? You need to be looking for a

Because *health* is your greatest *wealth!*

physician skilled in integrative approaches, blending "med school medicine" with alternative approaches such as The Yeast Syndrome. Most patients who follow my treatment advice get dramatically better – far sooner and far more than they ever expected could happen. Why not you, too? Maybe it's long past time for *you* to "Find it *now* – Fix it *right!*"ˢᴹ

A disease with many masks, The Great Pretender

You lose *every* time you don't try.ˢᴹ

Find it *now* – Fix it *right!*

Killing You While You Sleep?

"First, do no harm." Almost every medical student hears this caution from one of the speakers on the very first day of training, as they are welcomed into the fraternity of physicians.

Why, then, are we trained in the use of toxic medications and dangerous procedures?

The answer is more simple than you might expect: in order to produce meaningful results in people suffering from serious illness, body functions inside need to be "pushed around," and that task is *not* easy. As doctors, we dance on a sharp edge – falling off to the left, your patient doesn't improve and might even die; falling off to the right, your patient might suffer even more problems due to the treatment itself … and might even die.

Since we're trained to *"fight disease"* (that's the meaning of "allopathic" training, to become an M.D. – similar for D.O. docs as well), our focus is on drugs and operations to address changes as diseases are developing and progressing. What about actually preventing these illnesses? Or even *promoting* more robust *health* and vitality? Medical school is *not* "health" school, we don't get those strategies in our training.

Many people who are "in the know" wonder why doctors reach for 3rd and 4th generation antibiotics rather than prescribing older, safer drugs that could work just as well. I wonder, too.

Many people "in the know" wonder why doctors fail to prescribe drugs, or herbs and other supplements, or advise dietary changes to reduce the overgrowth of yeast when antibiotics are taken. I wonder, too.

Many people "in the know" wonder why doctors casually treat repeated infections every few months – sinusitis, bronchitis and even pneumonia, cystitis or kidney infections – or prescribe 3 or more series of antibiotics for a stubborn infection without searching to know the cause. I wonder, too.

Many people "in the know" wonder why doctors refer for surgery when easier and safer health-promoting alternatives are available, once you know the cause. I wonder, too.

These are obvious questions, and many more could be asked. But today I want to upset one of the holiest apple-carts of modern medicine. Let the apples spill where they may.

For whatever reason, your physician finds that your "cholesterol is too high." One problem is that studies sponsored by Big Pharma – the drug companies who make the medications widely

Find it *now* – Fix it ***right!***

prescribed – keep *lowering* what doctors can consider to be "too high." Fred Kummerow, Ph.D., published his studies for *70 years* on cholesterol and blockage disease. At age 100, he summarized his findings in a delightful book, **Cholesterol is *Not* the Culprit**.

Pretty soon, almost *everyone* will need to be "on" one of the many drugs designed to slam down your cholesterol level. At least, that's what *some* doctors say. Some people have even suggested adding such medications to our water supply, so all of us get treated whether we want it (or need it) or not!

But wait! Wouldn't it be useful to "treat" any "abnormal elevations" by directing our efforts to the reasons why? In other words … wouldn't we do less harm and more help if we just … *know the cause?*

Here's where this story gets really, really interesting.

Studies have shown that cholesterol can "wrap around" toxins produced by fungus and yeast (called "*myco*toxins") and reduce their damage to your body biochemistry. Does that mean that you might be generating higher cholesterol levels as an attempt to protect yourself from toxins produced by invaders intent on making a Happy Meal® out of you? More research might be very revealing.

I firmly believe that your body does exactly what it needs to do, as soon as it can and as long as necessary, to keep you alive and well. God didn't make any mistakes in this design. So ... why are we intent on crushing higher levels of cholesterol before we, as physicians, know the cause in each particular patient?

When your doctor "misses" the correct diagnosis, you are the only one who suffers. And, of course, your family and others. If elevated cholesterol is an unrecognized signal of fungal invasion and your body's battle against being consumed by The Yeast Syndrome, shouldn't you discover this ... and turn attention to repelling that challenge and restoring your immune defenses and other body functions?

In some (maybe many) patients, cholesterol is elevated in order to produce higher levels of Lp(a), which serves as a poor man's Flex Seal® to cover over microscopic injuries to the fragile linings in blood vessels. Why is this a "poor man's" solution? Because Lp(a) rises when you are deficient in Vitamin C – did you know that humans don't make their own Vitamin C, unlike almost all other animals? Linus Pauling, Ph.D., and Matthias Rath, M.D., showed these critical results in ... *the early 1990s!* But that's a topic for another commentary.

The drugs you are prescribed – *and* the true diagnoses that are *missed* and remain **untreated** – are,

Find it *now* – Fix it *right!*

indeed, killing you while you sleep. Even more worrisome are the later changes that we're finding: Deep Blood Fungus in patients suffering with many of the unexplained diseases that modern medicine treats with cortisone or chemotherapy, simply because those specialists don't know the cause. Happily, we're discovering complex treatment is producing encouraging results long after patients had given up looking.

Today's Take-Home Lesson: Find out what you need and demand it from your doctors … *or* invest the time and effort to find a physician who has the expertise to "Find it *now* – Fix it *right!*"ˢᴹ

The time is *now* to find ways to improve your health and especially to avoid *future* illnesses and lingering discomforts that yeast can produce, ones that steal your life and happiness. *All* of these can result from (or be worsened by) The Yeast Syndrome if no one ever shows you treatments and lifestyle changes that are critical.

You lose *every* time you don't try.ˢᴹ

Because *health* is your greatest *wealth!*

> ## You cannot heal in the same environment where you got sick.

Controlling the foods you eat and changing the microbial pattern in your gut create a wonderful environment for healing!

> ## Healing doesn't mean the damage never existed. It means the damage no longer controls our lives.

Properly *treating* The Yeast Syndrome means *restoring* more normal biochemistry that has been damaged by yeast toxins over many years.

You lose *every* time you don't try.[SM]

✷ For Women Only ✷

(and the men who love them)

THE *BEST* AND
MOST ***BEAUTIFUL***
THINGS IN THE
***WORLD* CANNOT**
BE SEEN OR EVEN
TOUCHED — THEY
MUST BE **FELT** WITH
THE ***HEART.***

— *Helen Keller*

Find it *now* – Fix it *right!*

At Least It's Not Another *Yeast* Infection!

Helen was relieved when her doctor returned to the exam room to report that he could see no yeast in the diagnostic smear. "So what do we do about my constant itching," she asked. The reassurance was a hollow one that she'd heard a dozen times before: "We'll get you a steroid cream and you should feel better soon."

A bit puzzled with her recurrent "personal" complaints, still she left the office hopeful once again. Her husband was encouraged to hear that this might be a quick fix. They had been missing out on too much togetherness due to her painful discomfort. Secretly, he harbored the nagging worry that his wife, looking somewhat older than her late 30's, was coming down with a much more serious illness inside. Helen had become a "complainer" in the last 5 or 6 years: belly pains and gas, bladder infections, a frustrating skin rash, and almost constant headaches. Many of her symptoms seemed to worsen just before her period, and the prescribed anti-depressants did absolutely nothing but make her sluggish and tired.

Sadly, her doctor was right – it *wasn't* another yeast *infection*. Helen's husband was right, too – she *was* suffering from a much more *serious* problem *inside*. And these two observations contain the entire secret as to why modern physicians fail to diagnose and properly, *completely*, treat ….. The Yeast *Syndrome*.

Seventy-five years ago, "health insurance" (which is really "*illness*" insurance!) was mostly unheard of. People worked hard, ate well, and didn't "run to the doctor" the way we do now. Back then, medical technology was simpler and costs were far less. So the question is … are we healthier today, with all of our wonderful scientific advances?

Doctors in 1945 had just a couple antibiotics available. Cortisone hadn't been discovered. Birth control pills didn't arrive until the mid-1960's. "Fast foods," which now make up more than a quarter of our daily intake, were only at the drive-in. Candy, soda pop, and other sweets were an infrequent treat. At the grocery store (no "supermarkets" then), mostly soup and Spam™ came in cans. And the environment was not yet as overwhelmed by poisonous chemicals and toxic heavy metals like it is today.

All of these factors can (and *do!*) damage your immune defense system. Almost all patients today have grown up in a world far different from that of their grandparents, even their parents. Unfortunately, our doctors haven't kept pace with the latest basic research, so many of them still have an "A-to-B" perspective: you come in complaining of symptom "A," and your doctor prescribes treatment "B." Couldn't be more simple than that!

Find it *now* – Fix it *right!*

Sure enough, if your test shows that you have "strep throat" (a bacterial infection that can harm your heart and kidneys), then the doctor prescribes a form of penicillin. Sadly, that's where it stops. You "get better" with the strep infection ... but the drug also kills the "good bugs" (Lactobacillus and other helpful bacteria) in your gut. Should you replace those microorganisms in your gut, after you finish the antibiotic? Of course! Does your doctor tell you so? Or how to do it right? Did you learn about this in your "health class" in high school?

Helen was suffering from a problem far more complex than her long history of simple vaginitis. After repeated courses of antibiotics for various infections – during which she was *never* prescribed a "yeast-killing" drug or supplement – her gut was overwhelmed with yeast and not-so-good bacteria. Since any of these can be seen in any "stool sample" at the lab, none of the doctors ever suspected an imbalanced yeast growth that was stealthily creating *most* of her body complaints ... not to mention her frequent moodiness, occasional depression, poor sleep, and loss of joy with her daily life. You can imagine the struggle facing her husband and teenage son and daughter – Mom was just "different" and not as happy as she had been years ago.

The various medical specialists were of little help. Her gastroenterologist insisted that she take an acid-blocking drug every day, now even available over the counter. What he didn't tell her was that stomach acid served as a first line of defense against infections coming in, including yeast in (or on) foods. And he didn't tell her that blocking acid meant that she wouldn't digest her meats and other proteins as well, leading to earlier aging and worsening disease patterns. Her dermatologist gave her cortisone (steroid) creams, which seemed to help … until the rash returned worse than ever. Pain pills were definitely not the solution for her headaches – but what was she to do? Her husband seemed impatient with her frequent complaints. None of the anti-depressants helped at all, and she couldn't tolerate the side effects. Worse still, her periods had become very painful, even for days before and after.

So was there a happy ending? We like to call it a "happy beginning." Helen came in after one of her friends said, "You've got yeast." "No," she protested, "it's *not* yeast!" What she didn't understand (yet) is that yeast overgrowth in her gut was seeping out chemical toxins *designed* to cripple her body chemistry – ***that*** is The Yeast <u>*Syndrome*</u>!

Successful treatment is *way more* than just "30 days of a yeast antibiotic" and "avoiding" sugars and starches. Proper care means finding and fixing the toxin-damaged functions inside: low thyroid levels, imbalanced hormones, impaired digestion, altered essential fatty acids so her skin and other organs couldn't repair and respond as they should, and so on. Her body was aging more quickly: she was hampered by toxic effects of the hidden yeast!

Find it ***now*** – Fix it ***right!***

Yes, you *could* call it an infection inside … but no one would ever diagnose *that!* Helen got much better over several months after she began a *comprehensive* program to address yeast and other health challenges. You probably haven't heard stories like this … but you would *hope* that she **finally** got better. *You* could feel better, too.

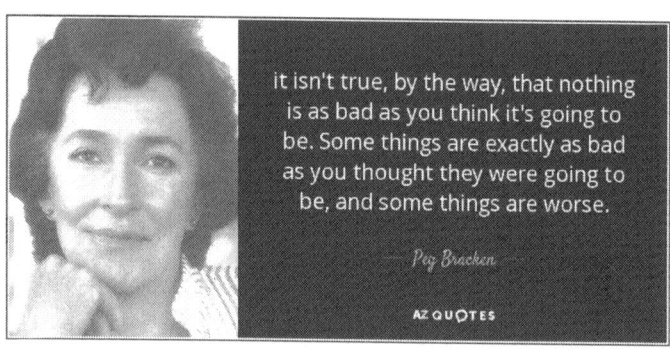

it isn't true, by the way, that nothing is as bad as you think it's going to be. Some things are exactly as bad as you thought they were going to be, and some things are worse.

— *Peg Bracken*

AZ QUOTES

You lose *every* time you don't try.™
Because *health* is your greatest *wealth!*

Heres To The Woman!

...Who knows where shes going,
And will keep on until she gets there,
Who knows not only what she wants from life,
But she has to offer in return.

Heres To The Woman...

Who is loyal to family and friends,
Who expects no more from others,
Than she is willing to give,

Heres To The Woman...

Who gives the gifts of her thoughtfulness,
Who shows her caring with a word of support,
Her understanding with a smile,
A woman who brings joy to others,
Just by being herself.

(Author Unknown)

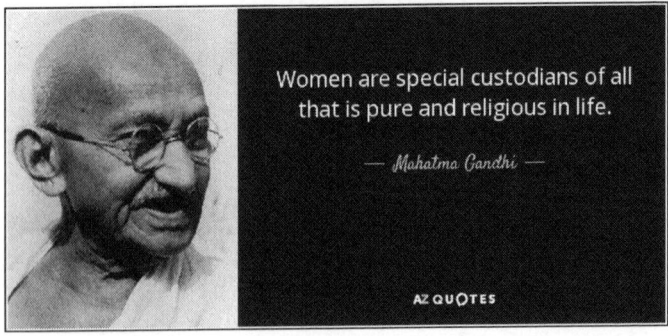

Women are special custodians of all
that is pure and religious in life.

— *Mahatma Gandhi* —

AZ QUOTES

Find it *now* – Fix it *right!*

Why Is It So *Hard* To "Treat Yeast"?

Kind of an odd question, since we have great drugs to "kill yeast," prescribed by most doctors to "treat yeast infections."

But … the *yeasts* are *not* the *problem!*

As someone who has a little bit of knowledge about this disease, you might jump to disagree with this bold statement. Pause for a moment: if we have such great drugs, why does my book – **THE YEAST SYNDROME** – give so much attention to eating plans and lifestyle changes? *Ah-hah!* You're beginning to ask the questions that your doctors should have been asking you for years.

Victoria's situation is typical of so many upwardly-mobile professionals who "shouldn't be getting sick" because they "pay attention" to their health issues (that means, they see doctors, get exercise when able, try to eat right, and so on). She is a pharmaceutical drug sales representative, covering a wide area of Texas, visiting dozens of doctor's offices each month. She had stumbled across **THE YEAST SYNDROME** book and realized that this might be an answer for her most troublesome problem – a positive ANA test ("Anti-Nuclear Antibody"), suggesting she could be developing an autoimmune disease such as "lupus" (lupus erythematosis, also called SLE – not good). Looking to marriage and children, the drugs that could be proposed for her in the future (cortisone and chemotherapy) were frightening at the least and she was seeking a solution not just a bandaid.

The job Victoria did daily was demanding: driving from office to office, often hosting the staff with treats or lunch, hoping for a few minutes to "pitch her drug" to the doctor. Sleep was a luxury for the weekends, since many days she was on the roads from early 'til late. Fatigue was a constant companion. Belly pains and headaches came frequently. Victoria had suffered for years with recurrent sinus infections and irregular periods – but what *really* got her attention were pelvic pains that might signal fertility problems in the future. Our first discussion centered on tricks she could use to avoid the quickly-available foods she sometimes had to gobble down, often while driving from office to office.

Certainly *you* don't eat "junk food." After all, that's candy bars and packaged snacks and sodas, high in calories and low in nutritional value. Sure, you eat at fast-food places (they prefer to be called "quick-serve" or "drive-in" restaurants) only when you're on the run with places to be, people to see. Thank goodness that "burger joints" and "taco stands" are located on every major corner – or at least an in-and-out convenience store! "Hurry, hurry, gotta get there." Sadly, any time you leave home,

Find it *now* – Fix it ***right!***

your dietary choices can become risky, especially if you have a full calendar.

Fast-foods usually provide few critical nutrients but are overcooked and high in sugars, bad fats, and salt. That's a formula for overweight, obesity, and *dozens* of "chronic diseases" (hint: *yeast*-related in many cases!). [Rent Morgan Spurlock's 2004 documentary DVD, **Super Size Me**, a real eye-opener that will change your viewpoint forever!] By contrast, healthy foods provide essential nutrients and energy to sustain growth, health, and life and genuinely satisfy your hunger. In "the old days," that meant "home cooking" for most Americans. The average American household now spends more than $3,500 a year on food at home and at least another $2,500 a year away from home. In 1970, we spent about 26 per cent of every food dollar "away from home"; by 2012, that amount skyrocketed to over 43 per cent. In 1955, there were just 9 McDonald's® locations; now there are more than 35,000 worldwide! ("Mickey D's" planet revenues in 2012 were $27.5 billion and it is the *world's* second largest private employer, behind Walmart®.) You almost can't avoid "eating out," even if you try.

Most "modern" folks, especially younger and even many middle-age adults, can't ever recall a time when almost *every* meal was eaten (or at least prepared) at home. As our lifestyles have become more hectic and our jobs more demanding, not only our food choices suffer but also our sleep patterns … our frequent need for antibiotics or allergy medications … our stress management … and pressures to succeed in every aspect of life. Victoria was no different – but she was alarmed by an obvious *downhill* trend in her health … and *she* was *only 25!*

Was The Yeast Syndrome her *only* problem? Certainly not – we discovered digestive problems from too little acid production in her stomach (more common after age 40), meaning that foods weren't being processed completely. Even worse, she had excessive permeability ("leaks") in her small intestine (so-called "leaky gut"), so poorly-digested food particles (even yeast and bacterial fragments) were sneaking in and banging on her immune defenses … a likely explanation for her autoimmune activation identified as a positive ANA test.

Find it *now* – Fix it ***right!***

Her evaluation showed low thyroid function (common with yeast – and often causing other systems to falter … such as ovaries and pancreas), even excessive levels of toxic lead and mercury accumulation even at her young age. Her pelvic pains were amplified by PMS and serious mood changes. None of the specialists had helped her to know the cause of her many symptoms. Until she began a *comprehensive* program to address yeast and other health challenges.

Was it worth Victoria's time to travel several hours every few weeks (then later, months) for our evaluation and refinement of her successful treatment program for The Yeast Syndrome? You could ask her whether she treasures having comfortable and normal female cycles, boundless energy, healthy digestion, clear sinuses, no headaches, normal blood tests. Or you could ask her husband – you might catch him more easily, since she's busy chasing around 3 healthy children (each breast-fed for months) while juggling her advancing career responsibilities.

Enough said!

You lose *every* time you don't try.℠
Because *health* is your greatest *wealth!*

Find it *now* – Fix it *right!*

"But Doctor, I'm *Still* Hurting 'Down There'!"

How many times have you heard this frightening conclusion: "Sorry, you just have to learn to live with it."

You *already* know how to live **with** it – you want to live ***without*** it!

Are you one of the millions of American women who suffer with a bladder infection each year? Dozens of thousands experience *more* than just a pestering discomfort or painful urination. What could be plaguing them?

Take your pick: chronic cystitis or urethritis (lingering bacterial infection *or inflammation* of the bladder or the short emptying tube), bacterial vaginosis (lingering bacterial infection in the vagina), vestibulititis or vulvodynia (painful outer or inner vaginal lips), lichen planus (painful thickening of genital surface tissues), even interstitial cystitis (intensely painful inflammation within the wall of the bladder). Any of these (and others) can blow apart any intimate relationship, since dyspareunia (*painful!* penetration) usually results as well.

Did you take your pick of what your doctor claims to have identified as *your* problem? Hold your horses … all too often, that's ***not*** "you." Sadly,

Because *health* is your greatest *wealth!*

many specialists appear not to have a clue, they simply can't determine the cause of *your* problem. And that, of course, is why they reassure you that they've done all that can be done – and usher you out of the office. Check Dr. Google, but don't hold your breath: "No one knows the cause …"

Simple question: why does a doctor who repeatedly doesn't have a clue about how to treat you assume that no *other* doctor has a clue either? As great as you think your doctor "is," what if he or she simply doesn't know about certain advanced treatments … or even successful "alternative" approaches that might provide the chance for you to become healed and free of these discomforts? Could that prospect even save your marriage or other intimate relationship?

So here's a special secret, just between us. You might be my *first* – but in 39 years of practicing "integrative medicine" (combining traditional training with "alternative" approaches), I am blessed that I can't ever failing to help a woman suffering for years with "pains down there."

Let's review some basics. Like the tissues of the mouth, throat, and sinuses, the female genitals have several moist folds delicately guarding the entrance to the vaginal vault. This transition area, from dry skin to moist surfaces, presents an almost irresistible invitation for microorganisms (especially yeast) to colonize. Body defenses include immune

Find it *now* – Fix it *right!*

system antibodies, a gentle surface rinsing action provided by natural secretions, and intact surfaces that resist potential invaders.

Challenges to natural comfort are many. By design and with the modesty of continuous underclothing, the perineal area (between the legs and including the vaginal and anal openings) is more tightly sheltered. Pockets of fluids can cultivate microorganisms. Chafing can abrade sensitive tissues, allowing superficial invasion. Bleeding with periods can change the local chemistry and pads or tampons can irritate tender areas.

Sexual activity (including with intimate articles), especially without adequate foreplay for lubrication or when prolonged or vigorous, can scrape or even tear any of the vulnerable tissues. The opening of the bladder tube (just above the vagina itself) is especially sensitive and pestering "urethritis" (inflammation, often without obvious infection) can easily be mistaken for bladder infection. Hormonal changes – whether from natural menopause or removal of both ovaries – often lead to thinning and excessively dryness of these perineal tissues, complicating all of these factors. Incidentally, petroleum jelly, some of the vaginal lubricants, and even condoms themselves or spermicidal products can seriously aggravate discomforts both inside *and* outside the vaginal vault.

Patients sometimes insist for their doctors to diagnose and treat based upon a simple urine specimen in the office – or even just a phone call: "Please tell the doctor that I'm hurting again." Urine cultures can *suggest* bacterial infection when none is present – or sometimes *miss* one that should be identified and treated. Specialists often rely on a vaginal examination, but inspection of the area *might* reveal little of value in diagnosing and deciding on effective treatment. Various swabs and cultures might be done, but again the conclusions *might* simply be misleading or wrong.

Where does all this leave you? Some women suffer for years. Even *decades*. Obviously there's no one simple answer, and certainly a brief chapter cannot make *you* well. My goal is to motivate you to search further for "the right answer" that heals *your* problem – and to provide you with some comfort measures immediately. Like, right now!

Douches are beyond a **no-no!** Unless, of course, you use a douche or enema bag with plain yogurt (organic, with live bacteria is best). Lie back in the tub, let the yogurt flow in, and do not rinse inside. A wet cloth or water from a pitcher can cleanse "the outside," then pat dry and wear a pad, held in place by panties overnight. Feminine "cleansers" are out! When you bathe or shower, just use Ivory, Dove, Aveeno fragrance free, basis, Miracle II, or a hypoallergenic soap, only for the

Find it *now* – Fix it *right!*

outside folds, *no* scrubbing just thorough rinsing and pat dry.

Most women do well with cotton panties, no synthetics, no pantyhose. (Ok, pantyhose if you must, but a good idea is first to put on panties and be aware for your personal comfort.) Here's an end-of-the-day comfort trick: make a body-warm water solution of Domeboro soothing soak (over the counter). Lie back in your tub, spread your knees, place a washcloth over your genital area, pour a few teaspoons of liquid over the washcloth, and just relax. Every minute or two or more, pour again. You may press the cloth gently against your skin and vaginal lips, but don't try to rinse inside. When done, just pat dry and put on clean panties (or just wear a robe or moo-moo).

Another trick for better health: moisten a capsule of high-quality probiotic (live culture acidophilus bacteria) and gently insert into your vagina. Again, no rinsing! If you prefer, you can mix the probiotic powder in with your yogurt douche.

You should be asking – "How would he know how to help *my* problem?" Let's just say that we're back at where we started: most doctors seemingly haven't a clue as to how to diagnose the real cause of *your* problem so they can't know where to start to finally fix you. Because I've been treating The Yeast Syndrome since 1983, there's a good chance that I do, really, *know the cause!*

Because *health* is your greatest *wealth!*   137

The list of infections (bacteria, yeast/fungus, parasites, even viruses) and inflammations (irritations caused by infections, exposures to various chemicals, allergies, hormonal imbalances or deficiencies, disease changes, and so on) is impressive. But *your* answer (even "answers," since problems often worsen like falling dominos) should be right around the next corner. So … I insist that *you* search until you see a doctor who *can find it now and fix it right!*

Would you like to give your doctor a headstart on finally fixing your problem?

I assume that I saw your head nodding "yes." So here's the key secret to share with him or her: you need *adequate* treatment for The Yeast <u>Syndrome</u>.

Sadly, your doctor just said, "I don't believe in that silliness." Or "quackery." Or whatever. Time for you to ask for referral to a doctor willing to work *with* you – not against you! – to do whatever it takes to finally resolve *your* suffering. Being insistent might be embarrassing at first … but are you willing to suffer in silence for a few more **years** just because *your* doctor is "*down on*" what he or she is not "*up on*"?

Besides, you might not be the only one suffering, depending on how your untreated discomforts are disrupting your life. If you can no longer tolerate sexual intimacy, the changes to your

Find it *now* – Fix it *right!*

relationship might be devastating over time. Bring along your significant other to demand effective treatment with you and *for* you.

And don't settle for the shopworn excuses such as "We don't really know," or "We don't try treatments that don't make sense," or "We don't do unproven treatments." Remember the doctor's job is to relieve and remove your suffering, not to commiserate with you and ignore treatments that he or she doesn't know about or doesn't agree possibly could help. Even if he or she doesn't know the cause, these treatments might be exactly what *you* need.

So what is The Yeast Syndrome and how should you treat it? This is a key concept: it is **not** a simple "yeast infection." Likely you've had yeast vaginitis once or more, sometimes responding to vaginal creams over the counter or requiring a doctor's prescription. A syndrome is a collection of signs (obvious changes) and symptoms (discomforts) that can be found together, related to a common cause. For most people, the common yeast in our gut (*Candida albicans*) has taken over, silently and secretly growing out of control due to antibiotics, cortisone and other hormones, dietary excesses of sugars and starches, unknown nutritional deficiencies, even unexpected toxic exposures to chemicals or heavy metals (mercury in your fillings would be a good example).

The Yeast *Syndrome* isn't a simple problem, and treatment can take several *months*, occasionally even a couple of years. Yeasts are sinister and terribly smart, so they trick and disable your immune defense system. Meanwhile, they fill your system with poisons (*literally*, yeast **toxins**) that damage your biochemical processes. Nothing personal, mind you – it's just business as usual for them. And the business they're about is to "make a Happy Meal®" out of you.

The more they damage your metabolism (that's simply what you do when you do *everything* you do on the inside), the faster you develop more symptoms and diseases … in other words, you become impaired, sicker, and die sooner. You might not realize it, but the "fungus kingdom" (yeasts, fungus, molds, and mildew) is designed to recycle the "plant kingdom" and the "animal kingdom." (We're part of the last one.) *Nothing personal*, just business.

You want to resolve all these troublesome infections interrupting your life, right? To treat The Yeast Syndrome and restore your body to better health like you enjoyed before, you need to follow a diet limiting sugars and starches. Over 34 years ago, I designed the intensely successful "MEVY" Phase I Eating program: *M*eats, *E*ggs, *V*egetables, and *Y*ogurt. Of course, it has to be adapted to personal needs. And you need to take yeast-killing medications daily, often for many months. How many? That all depends. The task is to

Find it *now* – Fix it *right!*

suppress/control yeast growth inside you for as long as it takes to *rebuild* your immune defense and other systems that have been damaged and are failing due to yeast toxins, nutritional deficiencies, and other environmental challenges.

A patient I'd been treating for over a year came in for follow-up. As we reviewed each of her earlier complaints, I made small adjustments as needed to her treatment program. When I asked about her lichen planus – a painful problem that had plagued her for years – her answer was simple: "That's been gone for quite a while." "No problems since?" "None." To understand the significance of her improvement … just type *lichen planus vaginal* into Dr. Google. I don't recall that we've ever missed getting someone completely better.

Vulvodynia? Chronic cystitis? Vulvovestibulitis? The names are many and confusing. But the answer is often simple – and it *always* starts with proper treatment for The Yeast Syndrome. Happily, a healing program can be quickly successful and can allow you to recover completely, with skilled and experienced medical management. Your discomforts can be serious and deeper than you might expect, rarely something for the do-it-yourselfer at home. You've already taken the first step: right now, you likely finding out about the cause and know that help is literally on the way!

Where do you go from here? Immediately go down on your knees and offer a prayer of gratitude that you have found a way to start on your journey to better health and even full recovery. Yes, I'm serious.

Then get more details in **THE YEAST SYNDROME**, my best-selling Bantam Book from 1986. Like just about every other topic that can be found on the internet, the quality of information varies greatly and you can be steered down blind alleys that fail to help you. The treatment program can be made simple – actually, that's your doctor's task, to work with you through any harrowing times. Trust me: you *will* have ups and downs, and you *must* keep your eye on the prize: *full* **recovery!**

As you have seen elsewhere in this book, many of your other body discomforts – rashes, belly bloating, constipation or diarrhea, frequent sore throats or ear or sinus infections, memory changes, brain fog, body aches and pains, the list goes on and on – might get a whole lot better with treatment for The Yeast Syndrome. Many people who have been trapped on the medical merry-go-round for years, spinning from doctor-to-specialist-and-back, stacking on drugs and operations, can suddenly find relief due to treatment for the *un*suspected problem that could be the cause of so many of their illness issues.

Aging is a *disease* happening one day at a time. Suffering with The Yeast Syndrome can make

142   Find it *now* – Fix it *right!*

your aging go ever faster, quietly stealing your vitality and enthusiasm as you begin to lose out in life. *And* your hope for relief in the future.

You *can* find treatment that really helps, *no matter* how many years you have suffered and *no matter* how far you fear your problems have worsened. Keep your eye on the prize!

Treating The Yeast Syndrome
means that everyone stays happy!

You lose *every* time you don't try.℠

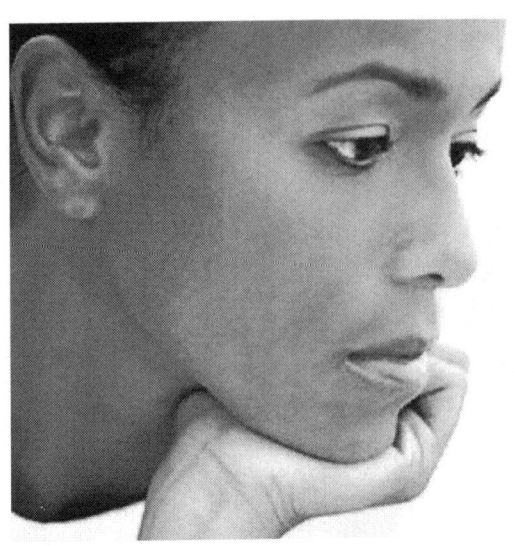

Every day brings quiet worries
when you or a family member
or close friend suffers with a
disease for which doctors
have no reassuring treatments

everything will be okay

in the end.

if it's not okay,

it's not the end.

Find it *now* – Fix it *right!*

Sneak Peek Bonus:

Treating Unexplained Illnesses Has Gotten Easier … and Better

Observations from

Beyond Cancer: *Jump* Outside The Box!
Treating <u>Un</u>explained Deadly Illnesses

forthcoming in 2018

Quick Questions

What tests have you had that never seemed to make sense to you?

What "diagnoses" have you been offered that never seemed to make sense to you?

Which family members or friends need to hear about these ideas now?

Other answers I am looking to find today:

You lose *every* time you don't try.^{SM}

Find it *now* – Fix it *right!*

Beyond Cancer: *Jump* Outside The Box!

Treating <u>Un</u>explained Deadly Illnesses

forthcoming in 2018

Lewis and Clarke blazed a trail from the Mississippi to the Pacific Ocean, opening new vistas for the westward migration of hundreds of thousands of "settlers" eager for a new start in life. Survival in these challenging environments was always at risk from what was eventually found to be bacterial infections. Pasteur later described that "germs" caused these diseases, giving us a hint on how to reduce the resulting death and despair. Fleming discovered penicillin then Domagk discovered sulfa, the first antibiotic drugs to kill bacteria inside the body.

Plant viruses were discovered by 3 pioneers from 1892 to 1898 – then Walter Reed in 1901 discovered the first human virus, the one causing yellow fever. Bassi showed that a fungal infection in silkworms was the cause of disastrous failures in the French silk industry. Earlier, Pasteur had shown that fermentation (making of wine or beer) depended on yeast. (It's ironic that these early discoveries about "infection" have now come center-stage with THE YEAST SYNDROME, *this* book *Sick and Tired?*, and

Deep Blood Fungus, all which relate to fungal/yeast infections destroying your comfort and health.)

A whole class of organisms different from the plant and animal kingdoms are *fungi*, which have been known forever and constitute the *third* kingdom of life. These include molds, mildew, yeasts, and fungi. They survive by "eating" the others, plants and animals. In April 2017, scientists announced discovery of a fossil record of what might be the world's oldest fungus, colonizing rocks dating back some *2.4 billion* years.

So what's *new* and *exciting* right now? We're forging forward daily, sometimes stumbling but committed to blazing an unexplored trail that is providing **un**expected **clues** for diagnosis **and treatment** of many (maybe *most?*) **un**explained, **puzzling illnesses** that cause untold suffering and death in our modern world. These startling discoveries came about because of an FDA-approved test, confirming DNA genetic sequencing of organisms found in blood samples, where comparison with the national registry clearly identifies *fungus* invasion.

Since the fall of 2015, we've been able to **positively identify specific fungi** found in the blood of patients suffering with a wide range of "inexplicable" diseases, such as …
>   **various cancers, blood cancers, severe
>   skin conditions, sudden kidney failure,**

Find it *now* – Fix it *right!*

sudden worsening of diabetes, MS (multiple sclerosis), ALS (Lou Gehrig's disease), RA (rheumatoid arthritis), SLE (lupus), other autoimmune diseases, vague immune defense system disorders, and others, including confirmed evidence of Deep Blood Fungus in the plaque blocking heart arteries (our *leading* cause of death) and in other body organs.

These last 2 years have been the most exciting in my medical career. I spent the first many years learning to ask better questions and gaining phenomenal skills in diagnosing and treating many common disorders. Truss described modern illness with yeast in 1978; Crook popularized that with his book in 1983. They are both gone now, but I have stood on the shoulders of those giants.

In 34 years of treating **THE YEAST SYNDROME** (Bantam Books best-seller, 1986), millions around the world have recovered better health and delightful vitality. I designed the first program to control "die-off" discomforts when starting treatment, and I have been blessed to discover efficient and successful treatments for people suffering with so many frustrating ailments, so they can recover from the pain of being sick and tired and *get on with their life!*

Like a pelican scooping up any variety of fish into his bill, people gather their own "personal" clusters of symptoms over the years and watch their health and happiness fade away as they visit "organ-doctors" (one or more for *each* problem area) who are clueless that an "innocent" yeast is poisoning their systems from the inside. A large part of the confusion is because The Yeast Syndrome shows up differently in *each* person – and can change in its presentation over time in the *same* patient, just like a pelican scooping up different fish each time he dives. But more ominous diseases are actually **killing** us ….. and modern medical science isn't looking at fungus as a root cause or contributor to suffering.

We are thrilled to offer our patients the hopeful prospect of *recovery from* – or at least *control of* – debilitating and deadly diseases where modern medicine has struggled to find drugs or surgery to help, in the face of no clear cause for these problems.

For many of these unexplained disorders, once that any kind of "diagnosis" can be made, **you** can be "stuffed into a cubby-hole" with others similarly afflicted. After that, you might find it difficult to have your doctors evaluate your new symptoms carefully, casually dismissing your pleas with the explanation that "People with [your illness] can suffer with [your new problems]."

What about treatments? Some have observed that "cortisone and chemotherapy" seem to be common treatments frequently offered, hopefully to control symptoms and provide some comfort. Think

Find it *now* – Fix it *right!*

this sounds silly? Ask your friends who have vague or serious illness problems for which no specific treatments have been successful – what have their doctors done differently? What effective drugs have they offered? What drug choices are offered over time? Recent advances in "immunotherapy" – drugs that can alter the course of serious illnesses – are promising ... but again, they are not aiming at the impact of fungal diseases as possibly stimulating the development of these unexplained illnesses.

Cancers, of course, figure prominently in our later years, as do heart attacks, blood vessel diseases, stroke, and dementia. In each of these situations, Deep Blood Fungus testing has been (you guessed it!) *positive!* When treatment has been pursued, in several cases the conditions have improved dramatically.

Is it possible ... that fungus infection *deep inside* your body could be the *cause* of – or at least could be *contributing* to – *your suffering and declining health?*

In many ways, we're having to rewrite the textbooks. We were taught that infection in your blood stream equals sepsis and you will die from septicemia. But that's exactly *where* we're finding what I finally titled "Deep Blood Fungus." These microbes survive inside a gummy layer called a biofilm, which shields them from your immune defense system … and probably reduces penetration of our drug treatments as well.

You won't find much on "Dr. Google," since we're actually writing the early papers on how to "find and fix" deadly and devastating problems from deep blood fungus. And, yes, we're somctimes surprisingly successful.

ARE YOU A CANDIDATE FOR OUR CARE? If you have pestering serious illness problems and you're sick and tired of not having answers that work … if you see the ads on TV for all the new drugs that are supposed to help these **un**explained diseases … if you fear that you're losing despite the best of doctoring, give us a call. If you fear that your life is slipping away, the time to call is *now*.

A SHORT LEASH! *If you're accepted* for care here, *we become partners*: you do *your part*, we do *our part*. We expect – even demand – that our patients take an active role … after all, it's *YOUR* health! We don't see patients often for office visits, so we expect for you to keep us informed of your condition and concerns. That way, we can "fiddle" with your program between office visits. *News Flash*: We've developed and are refining a unique algorithm (a protocol of specific steps) to help define the best treatment combinations for our patients. Like Lewis and Clarke, we're hacking our way through thicket and forest and paddling *upstream*,

152

trying to find "the way" to the West. (I started graduate studies in immunology in 1968, so I have a *slight* head start.) Welcome aboard to our canoe!

I trust this *sneak peek* has excited you about our forthcoming book, ***Beyond* Cancer: *Jump* Outside The Box!** The best news … is that you and your family and friends can benefit from these exciting discoveries right now, no need to wait for us to get the new book published. You can see hopeful healing vistas today: DIAL 1-800-FIX-PAIN.

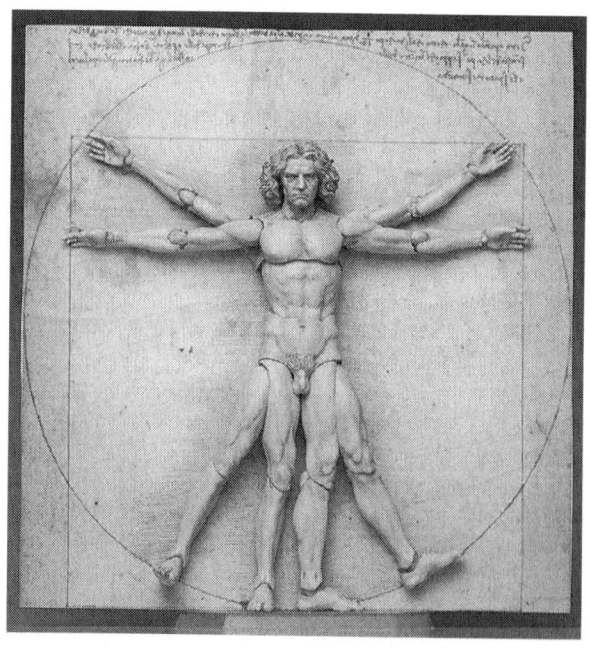

You lose *every* time you don't try.™

Hurricane Hell

Epidemics Of 2022:
Fungal-Related Illnesses
From Wet Structures And Vehicles
... Coming Years Later

Treasures of lifetimes, piled for trash pickup.

A million "wheels" destroyed by 2017 hurricanes.

Find it *now* – Fix it *right!*

Harvey, Irma, Maria ...
Strike With A Stealthy Vengeance

Escaping rising flood waters and finding shelter were the immediate emergency priorities during the violent attack of each of these storms ... just as with many prior hurricanes and with more to come. The stresses accompanying such massive disruptions to our lives are beyond compare.

Folks along the Eastern Seaboard, the Caribbean islands, Cuba, and the Gulf Coast have "weathered" water disasters for centuries – even deep inland cities such as Nashville have suffered dearly. Despite preparation and prayers, landfall storms wreak havoc in our communities. What people rarely realize are the later effects that can steal their health and threaten their survival in years to come.

As the waters recede and the overwhelming tasks of clean out and clean up get underway, trained medical specialists look, in the aftermath, for acute exposure illnesses related to fungal/yeast overgrowth. Such problems include irritation, infection, and immune inflammation in the lungs, apparently from inhaling spreading spores or fungus/yeast-produced toxic chemicals wafting through the air. Asthma and similar conditions can be triggered or worsened. Conventional medical care can be quite helpful for symptom control but many patients will require (and *not* receive) proper treatment for The Yeast Syndrome as well.

Damage to *all* buildings and vehicles is obvious: even ¼ inch of puddled water challenges the health of any structure! While owners with *minimal* intrusions might perform adequate cleanup and removal of mold/mildew/fungus/yeasts, many or most might have suffered damage requiring professional attention. Protecting those specialists doing the remediation (as well as surrounding environments) from contamination hazards becomes a high priority and protocols can be quite involved.

Suspect areas where "gutting and cleaning" might pose the greatest risk of remaining mold or similar growth include … cracks and crevices *under* the flat base plates resting on the concrete foundation, *in* the joints where studs attach to the base plates, *under* metal fittings and fasteners, and *in* unsuspected spaces concealed "behind" remaining structures, such as with electrical boxes and plumbing fixtures and fittings. Formed metal supports often encase a cavity readily penetrated by water and can host stealthy microbial growth for years. Even "weep holes" in outside walls can allow entrance into the structural cavities. Grooves in armored wire or other flexible conduit pose "impossible" demands for cleaning. Fireplaces offer special challenges with deep structures having porous materials and seams.

Find it *now* – Fix it *right!*

Most attention given to vehicles will be to restore and preserve mechanical integrity, such as with frame and suspension, brakes, transmission, and so on. However, interior floor zones, frame and door posts and cavities, side panels, and seat structures and materials can be similarly difficult to "sterilize." Any home, office, or retail furnishings can pose unique remediation challenges as well. Garages and other storage areas have cabinets and other structures that can harbor mold and other microbial growth and can be particularly difficult to clean, similar to many kitchens and bathroom areas.

But the *real "Hurricane Hell"* can surface *years* later – and take an enormous toll in human health and life.

You have seen that almost any discomfort, symptom, or impairment to normal function can result from poisoning by The Yeast Syndrome. *Candida albicans* is the responsible species for most people, since that is "our" common gut yeast. Sadly, as you have seen, most doctors simply miss the diagnosis … and therefore omit and never consider this essential treatment.

Many *other* yeasts, fungi, molds, and mildew can attack humans as well, with varying "success" and with wildly differing effects. So-called "black mold" is one that comes to mind, but there are others just as distressing. And often they are just as difficult to diagnose, so patients can suffer for years and worsen as their health disintegrates.

This chapter almost reads like a dry understatement, and you might struggle to "feel" the disasters that can befall many of those flood victims. Remember that *exposure to a contaminated zone is the key* – and that can come in totally unexpected ways. Examples include heavy rains and winds that breach the roof security and allow water into the attic and walls (even into closets), disruption of integrity of window mounts with penetration under the sill and wall, inadequate sealing or flashing where chimneys penetrate or at intersecting complex roof faces or building segments, undiscovered water breach of foundation (even under the fireplace), and so on. Never forget that interior leaks – sinks, tubs and showers, toilets, water heaters, HVAC units, damaged or disintegrating ducts, others – can leak water into the building structures just as easily as any major storm, from the attic to the basement.

Be practical: when you sense an odd or moldy "smell" in any environment or vehicle, arrange for expert evaluation to seek the source and determine whether salvage is possible. Remember ... if you ignore possible warning signs, later we might be trying to see whether salvage is possible for your *health.*

As a result of the severe hurricanes that battered Texas, Florida, Puerto Rico and other

Caribbean islands in 2017, stealth infections, allergies, or other immune disorders associated with exposure to fungal overgrowth or unseen by-products (toxins) can be expected to become more prominent within the next 5 years. (Scientifically proven? *No*. My best educated guess? *Yes*. Will our doctors realize how best to treat an increasing number of patients suffering with often puzzling problems? *Unlikely*.)

One other ominous prospect is looming: **Deep Blood Fungus**. This book is too short to offer explanations that will come in later publications. But an unquestionable statistic is that we are suffering with more and earlier degenerative diseases. In many cases that I've investigated, a "tipping point" can be identified, usually coming *just before* the unexplained diseases become apparent. This can be a major accident, surgery, illness, physical or emotional stress – and even overwhelming exposure to fungal spores and overgrowth. This last one is likely to be the stealth factor in the epidemics of puzzling illness that I fear are looming in the near future. Proper diagnosis and treatment could help you avoid chemotherapy, cortisone, and a myriad other drugs and operations for unexplained diseases.

What can you do to reduce the likelihood that you will suffer in this way? Take action steps to get your immune system in great shape, eat well, drink water, walk or do other general exercise, sleep long enough and well, reduce stressful circumstances in your life. These are merely general "preventive" suggestions – obviously the program is much more involved for older people and those already suffering with frustrating illnesses.

Could severe issues with The Yeast Syndrome *or even with Deep Blood Fungus* be threatening in your future? Pay attention to better ways to encourage more robust and rewarding health as *you* grow older!

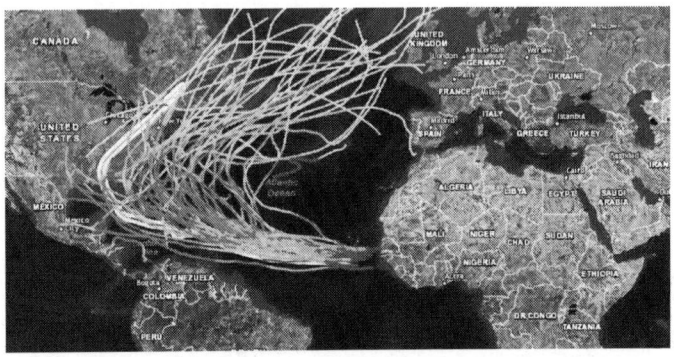

NOAA historical hurricane tracking map

My kind advice: don't be *hysterical*, and don't be *historical*. Get safely out of the way, even when that seems to be "crying wolf" once again. When you return to your buildings, carefully evaluate what risks might be lurking – and take every proper step to completely remediate any problems … or rebuild from the ground up, it that is what is required to preserve *your* health.

You lose *every* time you don't try.^{SM}

Find it *now* – Fix it ***right!***

Get Out Of Jail Free?

"Autobrewery Syndrome" Drunk *Without* Drinking

All right, so, let's talk about Too Drunk to Care because people seem ***not*** to be able to put things together until it just sort of passes a certain point, and *that* point does *not* have to be because they drank too much. It could be just because they're simply ***drunk***.

Whoa! Whoa! Whoa! How do you get drunk *without* drinking too much? Well, The Yeast Syndrome sometimes ***duplicates*** the condition of excessive alcohol intake.

The concepts are simple but generally misunderstood. By whom? By *doctors!* By *patients!* By *attorneys* who could provide the court with a medical explanation deserving treatment not jail. And, sadly by *jurors* and *judges!*

On the other hand, people and their doctors and their attorneys, jurors, and judges are going to be better able to deal with these issues more easily from now on.

What You Absolutely Positively *Must* Know

A "yeast *infection*" is a completely different kind of bird. It's an affliction well understood by doctors and patients, such as that the common definition in the vagina, or "jock itch," or "athlete's foot," even toenail fungus – but it can be *anywhere*, wherever the yeast-like fungus of *Candida* can grow. Once you eliminate the distressing infection, you'll still *have* the yeast (we *all* do, *all* the time), but it won't be aggravating you.

Oh, yes, many older people have toenail fungus … and they are *ripe* for developing The Yeast Syndrome. How to do they *get* frustrating nail changes? Well, generally they drop something on their foot, which injures the circulation right there. Now their defenses have limited access and don't work as well, and over time yeast gets a "foothold."

This is critical for you to remember: There are three great divisions based on energy chemistry inside – plant kingdom, animal kingdom, fungus kingdom. *Plant* kingdom takes sunlight, makes energy. *Animal* kingdom (us) eats the plants to get the energy or eats other animals that ate the plants. *Fungus* kingdom (fungi, yeasts, molds, mildew) *eats the other two*.

Which do you think is the smartest or certainly the most cunning of the three? After all, if

Find it *now* – Fix it *right!*

fungi (including yeasts) *fail* to overcome your defenses and to "chew on you," then *they* die.

And remember, yeasts are very, very sinister. They will literally make a "Happy Meal®" out of you. And *that's* what we are going to discuss. **You** won't be the "happy meal"? Well, you sure **will** because *you* are what's coming for dinner tonight. Under the microscope, yeasts are very, very innocent-looking. In fact, we find them in stool specimens all the time, they are part of the usual gut microbes growing inside each of us. So what does the pathologist's report read? *Normal* flora. And that's because searching under the microscope offers little help to doctors in determining the difference between "normal" or "usual" and *"pathologic"* even *"dangerous."* That's right – our physicians can have test reports that don't provide enough clues to understand a lot of things going on inside you.

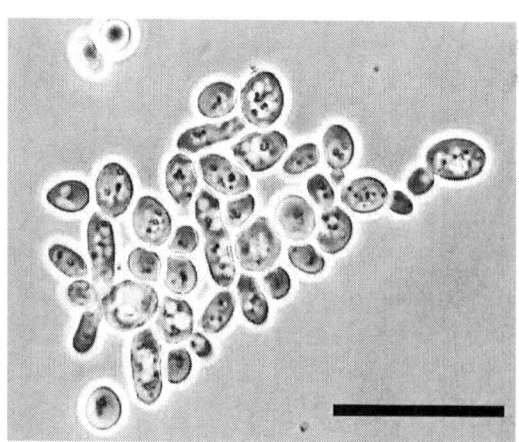

Here's what people who have yeast infections look like. Look through any magazine. Just regular people, like you and me. You know, regular people just get yeast infections. No big deal. Some infections are recognized, and folks search Dr. Google for answers and sometimes go to doctors for treatments. Others are less obvious. An infection might cause absolutely *no* symptoms and might be called "*sub*clinical." Just kind of smoldering along, these can cause unrecognized symptoms and skin changes might not be involved. Or someone might not suffer enough discomfort to seek any care … even though chemical changes can be progressing year after year. Sometimes these smoldering infections can create damage inside organs, especially in people with weakened defenses.

More significant infections, on the other hand, often in the *gut*, create The Yeast *Syndrome*. Doctors can have a huge struggle figuring out this deeper challenge to comfort and wellbeing. In case you were mistaken thinking that doctors are "real smart" and "think about things" until they get answers, let me challenge both of these conclusions. Your doctor has a zillion "sick" patients to worry about, a full schedule of patients to see in the office, maybe a dozen to manage in the hospital. There's simply not enough time and energy to learn about diagnosing and treating "everything," so attention needs to be concentrated on getting results quickly. For many unexplained diseases, that can mean

Find it *now* – Fix it *right!*

turning to cortisone or chemotherapy. Don't believe me? Check Dr. Google!

A *syndrome* is a set of signs and symptoms that can appear together. They characterize a condition, but seeing the pattern can be confusing. *You* do *not* have to have *all* of the signs and symptoms, but a careful review of your history, detailed examination of your body, and certain tests can be helpful to begin explaining what's going on.

Perhaps 30 to 50 percent of patients in America *have* (or are *now* developing and later *will* see) problems associated with The Yeast Syndrome. Why? Because we're in the richest nation in history. We eat more sugars and starches than anyone else. We have many foods that are lacking in needed amounts of vitamins and minerals, even amino acids and proteins and "good" fats. Why do we eat at a fast-food stop when we could have excellent home meals? Because we're rushing around in our daily lives. And fewer people even know how to cook! We have more stress and we're exposed to more toxic "stuff" than almost anywhere else. People get all sorts of health problems, physical as well as emotional (impulse or anger control issues?).

What does someone with a serious yeast-related illness look like? Maybe … just like *everyone* else! That's why your doctors don't see it. That's why people in general don't see it. *Almost nobody* sees it. They're just like "regular folks," except for tiny technicalities and biochemical disturbances developing and worsening inside. And finally they develop enough problems that they can hop onto the medical merry-go-round, getting worse and worse, finally getting diagnosed with this organ disease or that, this system dysfunction or that. And nobody sees or diagnoses the yeasts generating the poisons that are slowly killing us.

Many of us in our modern society are becoming ill as a result of our foods and our eating. Yes, they're different. We used to have gardens and farms, now we have agribusiness. Until the late 1940s, almost all foods were healthy "organic" – then we got fertilizers and pesticides and antibiotics, all of which are rampant now in our food chain.[7] Food selections represent our eating, and few people ever learn to prepare home-cooked meals and to choose a rainbow of vegetable colors (not just "white," like potatoes) let alone meats from animals raised without all the chemicals and processing. We have choices and we often choose wrong. "When you eat 'plastic' foods, you get 'plastic' people." In this increasingly

---

[7] Here's some "food for thought": An increasing number of patients *look* like they're suffering with an epidemic of "celiac" disease. That's a very specific medical (genetic) condition and is quite uncommon. However, many people feel dramatically better when they discover a need to limit their intake of *gluten* (found in various grains), so physicians and patients conclude "must be celiac" ... but often it's *not*. Instead, the most widely used pesticide in the world, RoundUp®, is claimed to have very low toxicity – but studies show that exposure can cause severe changes in your gut lining. Limiting grains, of course, can reduce your continuing exposure and many people feel much better ... even though they don't have classical "celiac" disease. Integrative medical approaches can do much to heal a chemically-injured gut, and that includes treatment for The Yeast Syndrome.

Find it *now* – Fix it *right!*

artificial setting, do you wonder why The Yeast Syndrome has come to challenge the health of so many of your family and friends … even *you?*

Photographs of yeasts do not suggest ominious – they look *so innocent*. But the toxins they produce are chemical poisons **designed** to *kill* you. Perhaps what *is* ominous is the overwhelming number of doctors who disregard the clinical evidence of people suffering with a wide variety of problems that often resolve, *disappear*, ***go away*** completely with satisfactory treatment of … The Yeast Syndrome.

The basic science studies have been published for years: yeast toxins are aimed directly at – and block the function of – vital biochemical process inside you. Simply stated, ***that*** is the method by which yeasts *eat you* from the inside out: damaged defenses can't defend, damaged organs can't work so well. Proper attention to the underlying changes can reverse the damage and restore more normal function, more vital health … *and* happiness.

If you have a disease, and your doctor doesn't diagnose it, do you still have the disease? That's almost like asking, "If you don't *believe* in gravity, do you *float* or *fall* when you step off a cliff?" Natural laws – like gravity and biochemistry – are quite a bit different than our civil laws. You can speed and *not* get a ticket. Did you break the law? Sure. Did you get caught? No. But biochemical laws can create serious damage and will "catch you" every time! When you have something causing your health to change, is that relevant? It sure is, especially if you have a disease and your doctor doesn't find it! Unless you get proper treatment, then you're going to get sicker, I guarantee it. And you depend on your doctors to find and fix your problems.

I have a patient with recurrent urinary infections. She listened to me about having The Yeast Syndrome and improved but she still had her urology doctor. I trained in urological surgery. She said to her specialist, "I've got to teach you about this," so she handed him my book and said "You know, I really think that this is what keeps causing my problems." He tossed the book back to her and said, "We don't read about things that aren't there."

Could her specialist be ignoring "natural law," the way things *actually* work? Then he's going to stay stupid. When doctors don't know something that's real, then they're simply ignorant ... but they could learn. When they refuse to learn, then they're arrogant as well. Know the definition of a dangerous doctor: One who's both ignorant *and* arrogant. As they say, "You can't fix stupid." Could be hazardous to your health!

One of the leading professors who set the stage for modern medical training and practice was Sir William Osler at Johns Hopkins University in

Find it *now* – Fix it *right!*

Baltimore. Most poignantly, he declared to students, "He who studies medicine without books sails an uncharted sea, but he who studies medicine without patients does not go to sea at all." As doctors, we have a duty to learn from our patients, to see what works and what doesn't. Often the most fundamental advances in medicine come from observing and listening to patients ... and then digging deeper into the science books to figure out the "what" and the "why." Certainly this applies to everything in medicine, including The Yeast Syndrome![8]

I get patients who want to change the way I want to treat and resolve their problems. Why would they even consider that? Most often they've found something through Dr. Google. I ask simply, "Did I write it?" If the answer is "No," then usually I don't care – because so many physicians and wanna-be's have merely a primitive understanding of how to manage patients with The Yeast Syndrome. For over 34 years, I've developed several of the unique programs that control the yeasts and restore body systems to more normal function.

---

[8] In the early 1970s, "high-fructose corn syrup" (HFCS, also called "corn syrup solids" and a dozen other *concealing* names) was introduced into our foods as a "sweetener." Generally regarded as "safe" by the Food and Drug Administration, HCFS is now an overwhelming additive, acting more like a drug than a flavoring. In 1988, endocrinologist Gerald M. ("Jerry") Reaven, M.D., confirmed "insulin resistance" (with climbing rates of obesity, diabetes, and heart disease) was due to excessive intake of sugars ... HFCS qualifies. In 1978, talented internist C. Orian Truss, M.D., wrote the first book on yeast-related illnesses: **The Missing Diagnosis**. Pediatric allergist William ("Billy") Crook, M.D., followed in 1983 with a wildly popular book, **The Yeast Connection**. These were my early mentors, who paved the way for my Bantam Books best-selling contribution, **THE YEAST SYNDROME** in 1986. Because *health* is your greatest *wealth!*

I *know* how to take care of this. That's *my* science of experiential medicine. Do I have the needed background to help patients recover? Maybe you should be the judge! Are these ideas readily available in the medical journals? No. How come? Well, consider this roadblock: we had a major medical conference in Atlanta in March of 2016, where key lectures discussed fungi and yeasts in human illness. We could not get approval for CME (continuing medical education) credit for attending because the "regulators" figured out that we were discussing what they consider out-of-bounds: "alternative medicine." Our dozens of references to basic scientific studies and documented patient successes meant *nothing* to the reviewers. Honestly? I thought that our job as physicians was to explore *better* alternatives … because if you keep doing it the same way as before then you'll keep getting the same (perhaps disappointing) results as before. The science of diagnosis and treatment marches forward by learning and employing new information, more than you knew earlier about how illness works and how healing happens.

About That *"Get Out Of Jail Free"* Card?

Let's get serious about "being drunk" *without* drinking. Or maybe "being drunk" with only 1 or 2 social drinks, not more. This really matters if you end up a courtroom accused of "driving under the influence." Your protests to cops and the court, that you haven't been drinking or you only had "1 or 2"

170   Find it *now* – Fix it *right!*

hardly matter … if you're there, then you're almost automatically guilty. That's why we have defense lawyers. But … what if your lawyer doesn't know that you might be suffering with The Yeast Syndrome and you need medical care and not jail time. Well, that's no different than your doctors who didn't know either!

"Carbs" are a concern, certainly starches but especially sugars. You might be trying to limit carbs but that can be an uphill climb. Sugar intake releases a neurotransmitter (brain chemical) called dopamine. That's the addictive signal for cocaine and other addictive substances … but sugars and starches are legal. *And* they're highly profitable to the food industry. *And* yeasts love them, so they might be "driving you toward" feeling that you really want to consume more and more carbs. *And* the yeasts can metabolize this stuff into … ethanol. That's *alcohol!* So … eating carbs might give you more than a dopamine buzz … they might make getting your brain "fried" (*drunk!*) pretty easy and you never touched a drop!

So let's take a woman of 150 pounds who consumes 9 to 10 or more drinks of table wine. She shows an alcohol concentration of about 0.30 shortly after consuming all 10. She'd certainly be drunk – that's over 0.08. She'd probably be comatose. She might get *dead.* That's serious stuff. That's a bigger dinner party than you'd like to think about.

A blood alcohol of 0.08 qualifies as legally drunk in most states. Your driving skills really get affected. There are criminal penalties past the level of 0.08. You face **proof** of being "legally intoxicated" and suffering criminal penalties when you pour down just 4-plus drinks. Death is possible at a level of 0.28.

How about a woman who drank *just 1 glass* of wine, maybe 2, at supper. All right, let's just give her the benefit of the doubt, likely she had "2" glasses because people often "fudge" or "forget" their intake. The case I'm presenting is interesting because her job was to host dinner parties for her company, so she had to remain sober. She often would tease at or drink a glass of wine to be sociable. She was found stopped at a traffic light with her head bowed on her steering wheel and her foot on the brake pedal ... **4** hours *after* the dinner party ended.

In response to questioning by police, she had no idea that she'd become intoxicated and she had no explanation as to why. Recall that she had only a "couple" of glasses of wine, maybe just 1. How could she become intoxicated – *drunk!* Interestingly, her behavior and conversation didn't suggest that she might be *massively* drunk.

Her tested blood alcohol level was 0.18 **6** hours *after* the party ended. Well, *whoa!* At *that* level and at *that* time, she should be documented as having all sorts of impairments with speech and

Find it *now* – Fix it *right!*

memory and coordination, attention, driving skills, judgment, maybe vomiting, maybe a loss of consciousness, certainly, an increase of risk of harm to herself and others. This is **6** hours *after* she finished drinking. But the police station video showed minimal alterations in behavior or speech.

How can we explain these contradictory findings? Actually, it's pretty simple to understand. Alcohol affects people based on size, weight, metabolism, food intake, and so on. That's why they put snacks up on the bar, to slow the rate of alcohol absorption from your gut ... so you can drink more without being as affected. That's also why they have a brass or wooden rail along the bottom of the bar (you see one in every Western movie!) – you can "hike up" one foot on the rail, that relaxes the strain on your low back so you can stand there longer ... and drink more. You don't stop earlier due to discomforting strain in your low back because you don't feel it. And after enough drinks, you don't feel it for that reason either!

When someone drinks an alcoholic beverage, about 20 percent of the alcohol is absorbed in the stomach, the remaining 80 percent as it moves further down into the intestine. When we start talking about the effects of alcohol, *nobody* talks about the bacteria and yeasts growing in the gut. Why not? The official medical position is that "fungal stuff don't matter much." The pathologist doesn't have to report anything other than "normal." He doesn't have to comment about it, even when more numbers are seen than usual. He doesn't even have to understand it. Remember, it's when you *understand* things that you'll get to explain more stuff about the world than you did before. That's the whole purpose of learning, right?

Understanding "Drunk Without Drinking"

Alcohol is generally absorbed into the blood relatively quickly. Medications usually metabolize slowly. Each drink can add a total of about 0.02 to your blood level. For every hour that passes you move up about 0.01. You can see that continuing to drink means that you're going to get drunk in coming hours or maybe minutes. Alcohol from any *one* drink (jigger, glass, or mug) can be fully absorbed within 30 minutes to 2 hours. That's interesting science because we can start "sort of" predicting blood alcohol levels … or how many drinks were consumed "when" … or both.

Your liver is responsible for metabolizing and removing alcohol present in your blood. Oh, wait a minute. What about someone whose liver function is less than it used to be, for a lot of different reasons. Our very toxic environment, several diseases, many drugs, even a history of alcohol intake – all these can reduce the efficiency of your liver chemistry processing.

Find it *now* – Fix it *right!*

Alcohol is removed from your blood at a fairly consistent rate: about a standard drink each hour or maybe little longer. That figures to be only about 0.02 at most. A 5'2" woman can "burn off" alcohol at about the same rate as a 6'1" obese man. All these generalizations are not necessarily true in every circumstance. It might take a bigger guy more drinks to raise his blood level, but remember that the actual measured blood level is then is what's going to dictate physical and mental performance changes for every person. Your brain doesn't care how you got there, only *that* you got there. Except there is an ... *exception!*

Knowing a blood alcohol level and the time that drinking ended allows us to make some simple "backward" calculations. We have to make reasonable *assumptions* about how fast the alcohol gets in and how rapidly your body can clear those concentrations. Certainly there's a large "fudge factor" here, but the blood alcohol level is a sure thing.

By "retrograde extrapolation" (making these assumptions and calculations, going *back* from a time and level we know), the young woman that I talked about could **never** have achieved a blood alcohol level of 0.18 by having only 1 or 2 glasses of wine about **6** hours before the blood sample was drawn. It just can't happen, since the laws of biochemistry are in charge. She has to be a terrible drunk and a horrible liar. She must have had 10 or more drinks at

Because *health* is your greatest *wealth!*

supper, by estimating how high her blood level would have gotten and then with her liver metabolism removing alcohol down to a level of 0.18 when she later was tested.

We're guessing at averages and variables and we can't *completely* pin down the facts. But you *can* closely estimate her blood alcohol concentration changes from when she was last drinking, based on her test 6 hours later showing a level of 0.18. At 8:00 p.m. she signed the receipt at the restaurant. Assuming a rise of about 0.02 in blood level for each of the one or two glasses of wine and a removal rate of 0.01 each hour, she should show *zero* as a blood alcohol level 6 hours later, not 0.18 (way above the legally drunk level of 0.08). BUT since her tested blood level was 0.18, and 6 hours of "metabolism" would have removed about 0.10 or *more*, her total "starting load" of alcohol would have been around 0.30 – the equivalent of consuming 10 to 12 drinks at the dinner party. If that were the situation, do you think that someone at the company event would have noticed her becoming stumbling drunk … or worse?

So how do we explain her predicament? Obviously she was "legally drunk" and was behind the wheel of a car on the public roads.

Two key factors *must* be understood. First, her history should confirm that she has suffered episodes in the past where she "didn't feel well" after a party or otherwise drinking alcohol. Indeed, that

Find it *now* – Fix it *right!*

was a common occurrence and she often "rested more" the day after, not understanding why she didn't seem to recover as quickly as others.

Second, and more important – *what if she really didn't drink more* than 2 glasses of wine ... how could she possibly show such a dramatically higher blood alcohol level? The answer can be alarmingly simple: yeasts growing in her gut gladly and *continuously* converted the carbohydrates (sugars and starches) from supper into alcohol, which was absorbed from her intestine into her bloodstream, gradually increasing her blood level in exactly the same manner as though she *had* been tossing down drinks a few hours earlier!

One other point deserves mention: how come she wasn't stumbling drunk with such a high blood alcohol level? This reasonable explanation leads to a conclusion that her liver and her brain have adjusted to seeing generally higher and even increasing levels of blood alcohol, possibly on a daily basis. This condition would be due to yeasts always converting dietary carbs to alcohol, more so after a greater intake at a party ... aided by the contribution of 1 or 2 glasses of wine. An unsuspected but continuously present minimal level would mean that her body has learned to "function" better than others are able when enjoying only occasional drinking binges. Does that mean that she'd be impaired during her usual days? Not necessarily – but she might feel less efficient or more "foggy" on some days, depending on carbs she had eaten.

Autobrewery Syndrome Is *Real!*

The term Autobrewery Syndrome describes these people who show the features of intoxication, not due to drinking but because of abnormal gut yeast proliferation and *internal production of alcohol* after eating carbohydrate-rich meals. This is the key point: drunk *not* because of drinking alcohol but because a *brewery in their gut* is freshly manufacturing alcohol from the foods they eat. (Starches are just "sugars holding hands," and your body quickly "cuts" the bond to make these sugars freely available.) Incidentally, unlike those in the back hollers of the Appalachians and elsewhere, this "still" inside you is perfectly *legal* but undesirable and, in fact, pathological.

How about the 2006 case of a 3-year-old girl with "short bowel syndrome," where normal digestion is impaired. She kept looking like she was drunk. A blood test indicated her alcohol concentration was frequently pretty high. Laboratory culture of her stomach fluid showed a particular yeast species, readily capable of fermenting carbs into alcohol, which then is easily absorbed from her gut. Parents (and hospital observers) confirmed an association between drinking a carbohydrate-rich *fruit* drink and her apparent "drunkenness."

Find it *now* – Fix it *right!*

Autobrewery Syndrome has to be listed on the differential diagnosis for frequent "drunkenness" or even abnormal behavior. Certainly for **un**_explained_ "driving under the influence." Anyone who's had sugar cravings really understands the intense drive toward sugar for meals and snacks. Could that be the yeasts "demanding to be fed?" Maybe, but someone with The Yeast Syndrome _can_ improve dramatically with proper treatment: many or most sugar cravings disappear when they reduce or remove carbs from their daily eating and control the abnormal growth of yeasts in their gut.

Consider someone on frequent or prolonged antibiotics. This can be the primary factor creating a significant overgrowth of yeasts in his gut. His doctor is not likely to notice something unusual. Even complaints of "gas" or "belly bloating" might be easily dismissed – or possibly treated with anti-acid medications, which further encourage the overgrowth of yeasts. In the case I'm describing, an elevated blood alcohol level was documented with his sugar-rich diet and taking an antibiotic. Just 24 hours after stopping the antibiotic and restricting carbs, his blood alcohol level disappeared. Repeating the antibiotic and having him eat sugars and starches, his blood alcohol level again rose. Such a provocative test might help confirm Autobrewery Syndrome in someone with similar circumstances.

A 24-year old woman admitted in 1982 to a UCLA hospital (Los Angeles, California) had a blood alcohol level of 1.33, *well above* that often leading to *death*. But she was alert and oriented. I propose that her body – liver and brain – had seen elevated blood alcohol levels for many of the hours of her life as an adult, maybe even as a child. Her biochemistry had accommodated to where her brain function is *not* massively depressed. Sure sounds like Autobrewery Syndrome.

A woman in upstate New York convinced the judge she hadn't been hitting the breweries. Her body literally had become one: Autobrewery Syndrome. According to the *Buffalo News*, she was stopped because of driving erratically. She claimed to have consumed only 3 drinks earlier and a breathalyzer showed a blood alcohol level of 0.30. In the first case presented in this chapter, our woman *would* have shown a level up to about 0.30 *before* she was finally tested. Both of these women can function in situations where you and I couldn't. Sufferers might not have a clue that they are carrying around a yeast brewery in their gut, just waiting for carbs to come in ... for a party! In many people, they're not even "thinking alcohol" because they didn't have anything to drink or maybe, as with our first woman, they drank only very little.

Classic reports from Japan confirm repeated attacks of alcohol intoxication. They appear to have different gut patterns of bacteria and yeasts. Many county or city prosecutors will claim that Autobrewery Syndrome has never been conclusively

Find it *now* – Fix it *right!*

reported *outside* of Japan. But remember that slow, continuous production of alcohol by fermentation in your gut over time can flood your system with higher blood levels, creating unexpected hazards harmful to both the patient and to society.

If this condition is never diagnosed by the doctors, then it won't be reported in the medical publications – so the only conclusion in the courts is that people driving under the influence are guilty of negligence or worse. But if someone doesn't understand what is happening and doesn't realize that he or she is becoming impaired due to an undiagnosed medical problem called Autobrewery Syndrome, then do they deserve jail or proper medical treatment?

What other medical condition do you know that uniformly affects *so many people* who could end up in a defense attorney's office? I don't know of any. Even "confirmed alcoholics" (we all know several) can resort to excessive (daily or binge) drinking due to chemical changes resulting from the Autobrewery Syndrome. They, too, deserve specialized evaluation, diagnosis, and treatment. The physical problems I'm presenting can be further complicated simply because yeast toxins routinely interfere with body biochemistry and can impair mental function, thought, memory, judgment, reflexes. These effects are above and beyond the contribution made by elevated levels of blood alcohol.

Because *health* is your greatest *wealth!*

Someone accused of driving under the influence can suffer punishment because their doctors are clueless, their attorneys are clueless, the judge and the jury are clueless – and the person himself is clueless about this special twist on The Yeast Syndrome. I attended an international seminar on fungus toxins in Dallas in June of 2016. About 100 doctors were there. Guess what? *Three* of us actually knew that I had written the book **30** years *earlier* – and that total of 3 includes *me*. How can we expect that regular doctors – even gastroenterology (gut) doctors – to know about Autobrewery Syndrome when self-declared "fungal disease experts" are themselves **un**educated?

Are you ready to share this vital information with your family and friends, some of whom might have "a drinking problem"? How about sharing with the attorneys you know? Keeping people out of prison and restoring them to healthier, happier lives by proper treatment of The Yeast Syndrome could have dramatic results for many years to come.

You lose *every* time you don't try.^{SM}

Find it *now* – Fix it *right!*

Now Review The Impact Of Failing Health In *YOUR* Life

You've taken the medications, you might have done special programs or even surgery. Maybe twice. But disturbing symptoms continue to steal your comfort and your capability – you are literally watching your life fade away while others go on.

Take a minute to reflect your daily or frequent discomfort. How long have you suffered? Do you remember when you first noticed you were becoming unwell? How did *that* feel back then? Did you have *any* idea that, years later, you could now be suffering even more symptoms that limit your life, your comfort, your capability?

Often we seem resigned to a false idea that aging is just "what happens." Aging is a *disease* that happens one day at a time. In many people, that disease might be The Yeast Syndrome … or, worse, the rise of Deep Blood Fungus. Our modern technologies *can* help restore your vitality, your enthusiasm, your activities in ways you might have long forgotten.

People – even or especially your doctors? – who know absolutely nothing about these latest advances are likely to be skeptical and discouraging to your interest in our testing and treatment programs.

The only answer is simple: get the facts, just the facts.

The warning in Proverbs 12:15 is so true at this important time in your life: "The way of a fool is right in his own eyes, but a wise man listens to advice."

We make so many choices that we hope will bring us happiness. Sadly, "stuff" rarely meets our needs – but we're often willing to make those costly purchases. True joy is sleeping well, waking rested and happy, going through your days more comfortable and more capable. Science now offers you a precious choice: effective treatment for The Yeast Syndrome – or, even more cherished, control of unexplained and deadly disease problems related to Deep Blood Fungus.

Find it *now* – Fix it *right!*

What we offer for your consideration are these opportunities that might be within your reach from our personalized treatment programs:

*   ***Could you see yourself feeling better*** than you've ever expected, to more fully participate in your relationships with family and friends?

*   ***Could you see yourself feeling better*** than you've ever hoped for, to more fully contribute to your work or your passions?

*   ***Could you see yourself feeling better*** than others have ever expected, to engage your life with robust vitality, able to share more of a hopeful future, looking forward to living longer, more comfortable, more capable?

We offer these prospects to each and every one who qualifies to be our patient. Those who take our programs seriously often are surprised to find that we meet these objectives and beyond. The choice, as always, is yours. We simply say, "Keep your eye on the prize … you deserve a brighter future now."

Take Home Lesson: Infections cause many of our discomforts and diseases – finally, we can treat many unexplained problems rather simply surrendering to the suffering.

You lose ***every*** time you don't try.℠

Because *health* is your greatest *wealth!*   185

The effort *might* seem "too much" at the start …

But the view from the "peak of your health"
is breathtaking. And we'll be here to help you!

Find it *now* – Fix it *right!*

Are You Ready To Make The Call?

Because *health* is your greatest *wealth!*

DIAL 1-800-FIX-PAIN

Your only "cost" is just a few minutes ...

And what you gain could be *priceless!*

You lose *every* time you don't try.℠

Find it *now* – Fix it *right!*

Finding Answers In
THE YEAST SYNDROME
Bantam Books Best-Seller

Order *your* copy now from amazon:

Find these topics starting on pages noted:

Because *health* is your greatest *wealth!*

You lose *every* time you don't try.^{sm}

Find it *now* – Fix it *right!*

Life Celebrating Health

9816 Memorial Blvd – Suite 205
Humble – Texas
DIAL 1-800-FIX-PAIN
www.healthCHOICESnow.com

What We Can Do For You …

The easiest way to explain our services is simply that we can help you to feel better, to feel younger, to feel more vital and optimistic in your life, when we **"Find it *now* – Fix it *right!*"**ᔆᴹ

Correct diagnosis is critical – correct treatment is essential! Dr. Trowbridge has trained for 45 years to *look for* and *treat* the **cause** of your problems, not just slap on another fancy bandaid. Sadly, many doctors don't have the time or perhaps even the experience to recognize deeper reasons why you are suffering … then to design safe, effective, often natural solutions.

An Eagle Scout, National Merit Scholar, and California State Scholar, Dr. Trowbridge graduated from Stanford University and Case Western Reserve School of Medicine. Exceptional training opportunities in medical and surgical approaches helped shape his "big picture" views of resolving illness and restoring health. Respected for his incisive thought and broad perspectives, Dr. T's career accomplishments are recognized in over 5

Because *health* is your greatest *wealth!*

dozen volumes of ***Who's Who*** – and by being named a Fellow of the American College for Advancement in Medicine (FACAM) – and by being honored by his colleagues with the Distinguished Lifetime Achievement Award from the International College of Integrative Medicine.

Best-selling author of several books, Dr. Trowbridge lectures across the country and around the world. He has authored several invited articles on integrative treatments for the *Townsend Letter* and on various topics for other journals and newsletters.

Dr. T has served as president, chairman, officer, director, or advisor to the board of several professional associations, among these are the International College of Integrative Medicine, the International Academy of Biological Dentistry and Medicine, the American College for Advancement in Medicine, and the National Health Federation.

His devotion to patient education has resulted in several books, radio shows, CDs, and DVDs. Most notable is his million-copy best-selling Bantam Book **THE YEAST SYNDROME** – in many circles he's long been known at "The Yeast Doc."

Launched in 2017 was **Mastering the Art of Success** with Jack Canfield of the *Chicken Soup for the Soul* series, which hit 3 amazon best-seller lists in the first 18 hours. Dr. T's chapter won the Editor's Choice Award. Another recent launch was

DRIVEN! with internationally acclaimed motivational speaker/author Brian Tracy, which scored as an amazon best-seller in its first day. Again, Dr. T's chapter won the Editor's Choices Award. Forthcoming in 2018 is a chapter in **The Big Question** with world-famous radio and television host Larry King.

Get your copies of these excellent books now: **Mastering the Art of Success**

And Brian Tracy's book ***DRIVEN!***

Also published in 2017 is Dr. T's equally popular book on using unique "stem cells" (from a federally-registered tissue bank) to help relieve long-standing pain and limitation, **Failure is *not* an Option**. Get your copy at amazon as well:

Because *health* is your greatest *wealth!*

To complement *this* book that you're reading right now, you'll want to include in your home library a copy of **THE YEAST SYNDROME**, which you will come to depend on for years to come, to regain and maintain your health:

Coming soon in 2018 is
Second Chance

... for those who survived their first heart attack and those *want* to.

An incredibly successful FDA-approved drug treatment program to reduce toxic metals and improve health – Chelation Therapy – has been largely ignored by the medical community and by the media, so it remains unknown to the general public. Hardly anyone is aware that results of a large National Institutes of Health study, reported in 2012,

Find it *now* – Fix it *right!*

showed that chelation reduces second heart attacks …
and it works twice as well in diabetics! (Available
this winter from amazon.com)

Also planned for later 2018 will be
**HEARTBROKEN: Top 5 Reasons To Doubt
Your Heart Doctor**, the flagship volume (on
diagnosis and treatment of heart disease) in his new
DOUBT YOUR DOCTOR™ book series. These
publications will give readers easy-to-understand
guidelines by which to review whether their
specialists are providing the care they really need.
People have longed turned to Dr. Google in
frustration; these books covering various diseases and
body systems will help steer them in all the right
directions. Well-respected integrative medicine
experts in various specialty topics will spearhead the
volumes in this series.

Also forthcoming will be an incredibly
valuable book that reviews newly-discovered and
often successful treatments for unexplained deadly
illnesses apparently caused or at least worsened by
Deep Blood Fungus:
Beyond **Cancer: *Jump* Outside The Box**
Since the fall of 2015, we've been able to *positively
identify specific fungi* found in the blood of patients
suffering with a wide range of "inexplicable"
diseases, such as …

**various cancers, blood cancers, severe
skin conditions, sudden kidney failure,
sudden worsening of diabetes, MS**

(multiple sclerosis), ALS (Lou Gehrig's disease), RA (rheumatoid arthritis), SLE (lupus), other autoimmune diseases, vague immune defense system disorders, and others, including confirmed evidence of Deep Blood Fungus in the plaque blocking heart arteries (our *leading* cause of death) and in other body organs.

Dr. T's present clinical research interests also include exploring the best procedures for using our "stem cells" to help patients suffering with pain; improvement or control of atrial fibrillation rhythms by non-drug treatments; accelerated healing with advanced natural prolotherapy (tissue growth stimulating) injections for patients with joint injuries, neck and back pains, and arthritis; and advanced treatment strategies to manage and prevent cardiovascular disease, especially congestive heart failure and recovery from heart attacks, strokes, peripheral arterial disease and gangrene, and diabetic ulcers and neuropathy.

We invite you to browse our website to learn more about the many treatment programs we offer to help you, your family, your friends:

www.healthCHOICESnow.com   or scan ...

Find it *now* – Fix it *right!*

Under construction/coming soon:
stem-cells-usa.com   or scan ...

Our new site will be a valuable resource for you in coming months and years.

Here's our little secret: Right now, you can download and print a ***free*** pdf copy of ***Sick and Tired?*** from this webpage:

www.healthCHOICESnow.com/sick-and-tired
or scan ...

Because *health* is your greatest *wealth!*   197

when you get
sick and tired
of being
sick and tired~
you will change

aprilp.com

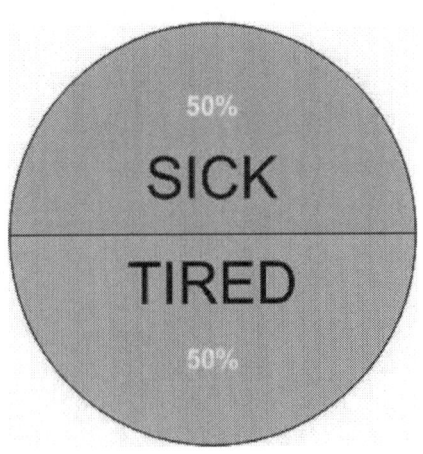

Find it *now* – Fix it ***right!***

What Symptoms *Could*
THE YEAST SYNDROME
Create Inside You?

The story gets "tricky" in terms of trying to pin down whether *you* might be suffering with The Yeast Syndrome. There is no "one" collection of symptoms that is conclusive, so the very **same** diagnosis (of "yeast") can be offered to ten patients in a row, each presenting with dramatically different complaints. Lab test reports require careful interpretation in order not to miss the damage this condition is doing to immune defenses. This puzzling condition can destroy your health and happiness while it can masquerade as – or biochemically create – disorders (disturbed function) in *each and every* organ system, where the deeper underlying cause is very often missed by conventional doctors.

You might find the following list of "**common**" symptoms useful in helping to determine whether you could have – and could benefit from proper treatment of – The Yeast Syndrome.

Uncommon ones, just like these "common" ones, are usually missed as diagnoses related to yeast overgrowth … so *they* are **not** treated either!

fatigue, malaise ("the blahs"), or weakness
exhaustion, especially after any exertion

brain fog, focus or concentration or memory issues
ADD/ADHD concentration issues, even as adult
irritability or mood swings
lightheadedness or dizziness
sensitivity to light, sounds, temperature
anxiety, depression, or both
belly bloating
heartburn
constipation or diarrhea – or both, back and forth
recurring nausea
recurring vaginal yeast infections
recurring urinary bladder/kidney infections
recurring breakouts/inflammation/irritation/itching
recurring "jock itch" groin infections
recurring athlete's foot, peeling/cracking skin on feet
persistent yellowing/fungus infections of toenails
persistent dry skin/rash (eczema)
itching ears or other skin areas
recurring hives/allergy skin reactions
oral thrush or discolored tongue
halitosis (bad breath)
recurring sinus or ear infections
frequent need for antibiotics for various conditions
recurring "strep" throat or other "colds"
recurring "cold sores"
food allergies or intolerances
altered immune system/frequent illnesses
indigestion requiring drugs – or not getting better
unexplained or worsening joint pains
"autoimmune" joint or muscle pains (RA rheumatoid
          arthritis, SLE lupus arthritis)
other "autoimmune" changes such as thyroiditis,

Find it *now* – Fix it ***right!***

ulcerative colitis/Crohn's colitis, scleroderma,
psoriasis, even MS multiple sclerosis, ALS
recurring flu-like symptoms
enlarged lymph nodes
weight changes, up or down
cravings for sugars or starches or alcohol
diabetics or pre-diabetics at higher likelihood
users of oral contraceptives at higher likelihood
users of steroid/cortisone drugs at higher likelihood
users of antibiotics at higher likelihood
higher stress circumstances at higher likelihood
sleep disturbances at higher likelihood
various disease sufferers at higher likelihood,
especially when drugs encourage fungus
hormone imbalances, even when not older
decrease or loss of sex drive or performance

various symptoms worsening in damp or humid
environments, especially if "moldy" smelling

The list could go on for many pages … but
you get the idea! When puzzling problems continue
to make your life more uncomfortable, *always*
consider that The Yeast Syndrome might be a major
contributing factor – and proper treatment might the
key to a brighter, healthier future.

You lose *every* time you don't try.[SM]

The easiest way to share exciting new, health-restoring information with your family and friends is to have them read and explore our extensive educational materials on their own, so they too will discover that they truly have health **CHOICES** now!

Feel free to share: www.healthCHOICESnow.com

You lose *every* time you don't try.℠

Find it *now* – Fix it *right!*

What Kind Of Specialists *Could* "Treat" The Yeast Syndrome?

Family Practice – unless they don't know about it or about how to properly treat it completely

Internal Medicine – unless they don't know about it

Ear/Nose/Throat (Otorhinolaryngology / sinuses) – unless they don't know about it

Infectious Disease – unless they don't know about it

Pulmonology (Lung) – unless they don't know about it

Dermatology (Skin) – unless they don't know about it

Gastroenterology (Gut) – unless they don't know about it

Endocrinology (Glands) – unless they don't know about it

Gynecology (Female Organs) – unless they don't know about it

Urology (Kidneys/Bladder) – unless they don't know about it

Neurology (Brain/Nervous System) – unless they don't know about it

Rheumatology (Joints/*Medical*) – unless they don't know about it

Orthopedics (Joints/*Surgical*) – unless they don't know about it

Podiatry (Feet/Ankles/D.P.M.) – unless they don't know about it

Integrative – Functional – Complementary – Alternative (Physician "doing it differently") – unless they don't know about it

Naturopathy (Natural Medicine/N.D.) – unless they don't know about it

Chiropractic (Spinal Manipulation/D.C.) – unless they don't know about it

M.D. = "regular" medical school
D.O. = osteopath = "regular" medical school with
        emphasis on body structure and joints
D.P.M. = "podiatry" foot/ankle medical/surgical school
N.D. = "natural medicine" school (without drugs/surgery)
D.C. = "chiropractic spinal manipulation" medical school
        (without drugs/surgery)

A search of "Dr. Google" (you know, **google.com**, relied on by everyone as providing instant diagnoses and definitive second opinions!) shows over 291,000 "hits" when searching for "yeast syndrome." **PubMed.com**, the government internet index of journal articles on medical and basic science topics, does *not* list "yeast syndrome" but includes over 34,000 papers under the category of "candidiasis" and 9 under "candida syndrome." Sadly, many *more* monthly articles are *omitted* from PubMed/MEDLINES than are included – making their observations much harder to find. (The director who oversaw writing of the MEDLINES computer search program kindly taught me advanced search strategies when I was at the National Institutes of Health in 1976. *That* gave me some wonderful unique tools!)

One scholarly-sounding report in 2002 concludes, after "systematic review" of 96 *qualifying* studies, that "Nevertheless, neither epidemiological nor therapeutic studies provide evidence for the existence of the so-called "Candida-syndrome" or "Candida-hypersensitivity-syndrome". At present, there are no proven treatment indications for antifungal "bowel decontamination".[9] Like the experts at the International Mycotoxin Symposium in Dallas, Texas, in June 2016 – *they* haven't read my book.

You lose *every* time you don't try.ˢᴹ

---

[9] Lacour M et al, Int J Hyg Environ Health. 2002 May;205(4):257-68.
Find it *now* – Fix it ***right!***

Why *Could* You Feel Tired?

Obviously no book can diagnose any one person BUT sometimes a list can offer ideas you might not have considered. You could look up any of the following on Dr. Google and discuss your concerns with your personal physician. Please do *not* take up valuable office visit time questioning about rare and *unlikely* problems ... unless *specific* reasons make them more likely to explain *your* suffering!

Common (almost *obvious!*) Causes ...

inadequate length or poor quality sleep
"sleep apnea" (including snoring)
inadequate amount or poor quality food intake
anemia (low red blood cell counts, all reasons)
depression
obesity/overweight
metabolic syndrome (insulin resistance)
hypothyroidism (even with "normal" blood tests)
caffeine overload (coffee, tea, some soft drinks)
undiscovered smoldering urinary infection
diabetes/sugar intolerance
dehydration
heart diseases (various, known or developing)
work sleep disorder ("shift" work)
food (or other chronic exposure) allergies
chronic fatigue syndrome ("fibromyalgia")

Sometimes *Overlooked* Causes …

hypotension (lower than desirable blood pressures, as
       with adrenal fatigue or dysfunction)
hypotension (overly aggressive medications)
heart muscle contractility or rate/rhythm disorders
alcohol use or abuse
sedative use or abuse (especially soporifics/sleep)
allergy treatments (antihistamines, cough drugs)
jet lag / travel stress
corticosteroid use
aggressive exercise
sedentary lifestyle ("couch potato")
lower brain blood flow (as with blockage of neck
       carotid arteries or brain cerebral arteries)
anti-cancer treatments ("chemo" or radiation)
cancers of various kinds (known or developing)
kidney disease (sudden or chronic)
liver failure (sudden or chronic)
low blood oxygen levels ("COPD," bronchiectasis,
       interstitial pulmonitis, central or obstructive
       sleep apnea, mismatch of tongue and jaw
       size, spine kyphosis/hump or scoliosis)
low blood oxygen levels (acute, such as "altitude
       sickness," pneumothorax, tracheal puncture)
hyperthyroidism (especially autoimmune thyroiditis)
MS (multiple sclerosis, brain/spinal cord damage)
ALS (Lou Gehrig's disease, brain/spinal cord
       disorder)
Parkinson's disease (brain degeneration disorder)
myasthenia gravis (specific muscle weakness)
mass lesion (any swelling) *inside* the skull

Find it *now* – Fix it *right!*

TBI / traumatic brain injury (concussion)
hypopituitarism ("master gland" dysfunction)
hypercalcemia (high blood calcium, all causes)
Alzheimer's disease (?diabetes type III?)
headaches (all causes and kinds)
whiplash neck injury (all chronic muscle strains)
PMS / premenstrual syndrome
menstrual (period) difficulties or discomforts
hormone imbalances (men or women, *all* kinds)
depression postpartum (after delivery)
SAD ("seasonal affective disorder")
grief or worry (sudden or longer lasting)
excessive use of "brain drugs" (as antidepressants,
        anxiety relievers, antipsychotics)
excessive use of pain relieving drugs
chronic pain syndromes (all kinds)
Munchausen syndrome (malingering, pretending)
"secondary gain" situations (unconscious
        psychological motivations)
stress (acute or recurrent or chronic)
cognitive (thinking) impairment
maldigestion / malabsorption syndromes
inflammatory bowel diseases
mitochondrial dysfunctions (genetic or new)
occult (hidden/undiscovered) infections (bacterial,
        viral, fungal, parasitic, especially deep jaw)
vitamin B_{12} deficiency
folic acid deficiency
vitamin D_3 deficiency
autoimmune disorders (*all* kinds, *all* organs)
muscle wasting diseases
"statin" (anti-cholesterol) or similar drugs

antihypertensive drugs (likely when multiple used)
electrolyte imbalances (sodium, magnesium, others)
proton pump inhibitors (acid-blocking drugs)
some antibiotics
gut bacterial disturbances (microbiome imbalance,
        "SIBO," especially due to antibiotics)
psychiatric ("mental") illness (all kinds)
spiritual crisis
toxic metal body burden (rarely suspected)
toxic chemical exposures (rarely suspected)
toxic mold chemical exposures ("VOCs," volatile
        organic compounds, rarely suspected)
diffuse brain blood vessel blockages (microvascular
        occlusions, "tiny" strokes)
TIAs (transient ischemic attacks, "come-and-go
        strokes")
heart-lung pump syndrome (after heart operations)
general anesthesia exposure (varies wildly)
... and several other possible causes not even listed!

Add your own experiences or observations ...

… and always include

The Yeast Syndrome
and / or
Deep Blood Fungus

as possibilities to be considered *whenever* fatigued,
for whatever other reasons ... many different disease
issues can "invite" others to come along together!

Remember that *your children* could suffer similarly.

You lose *every* time you don't try.^{SM}

Find it *now* – Fix it *right!*

To quickly order extra copies of this book
Sick and Tired?
to share with family and friends
sent direct to you from amazon.com …

simply scan …

If you also want to order your own copy of
Bantam Books best-seller
THE YEAST SYNDROME
or copies to share with family and friends …

Remember that these are
"personal workbooks," for you to make notes
that help you see *your way* to better health!

You lose *every* time you don't try.℠

Because *health* is your greatest *wealth!*

Your way to healthy
easier than getting to the City of Oz!

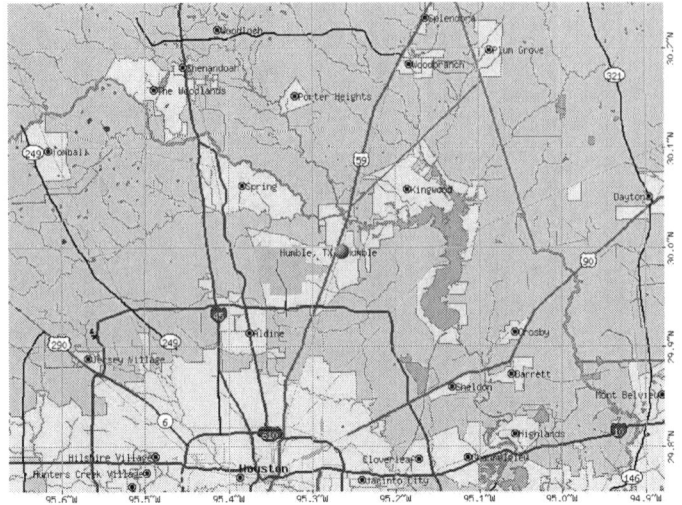

Humble is directly in the **center** of this map.
From _Houston_ – come north on US 59/I-69,
take the "Humble / FM 1960" exit and "loop under"
the highway to come southbound on the feeder road,
pass Toyota, turn right toward the hospital,
we're in the *first* red brick building
on your left – 9816 ... on the second floor.

From the _north_, take the "Will Clayton /Airport" exit
and *quickly* get over to turn right toward the hospital.

From the _east_ (Lake Houston), come west on FM 1960,
turn *left* at US 59/I-69 and stay on the southbound feeder,
pass Toyota, turn right toward the hospital.

From the _west_ (Spring), come east on FM 1960,
turn *right* at US 59/I-69 and stay on the southbound feeder,
pass Toyota, turn right toward the hospital.

Find it *now* – Fix it *right!*

We're Ready To
Make *Your* Life Great Again!

Dr. T – as he's been known since 1978 in our office – does "some" of the work … but we're thrilled to do all of the rest for you. Our staff of 6 is lead by two of us who've been here 27 years each – our next junior assistant for almost 13 years. The others are "newbies," from 6 years on down. And we're all trained and excited and committed to helping him everyday: **"Find it *now* – Fix it right!"**[SM]

Send us your questions:
　　　　　info@healthCHOICESnow.com
Fax us your questions: 281-540-4329
Call us with your questions: DIAL 1-800-FIX-PAIN

We work diligently to get you the "right answers" as soon as possible. *And* we invite you to come visit us face-to-face and talk with our patients too! We're easy to find: a 2-story red brick building right across the street from the Memorial Hermann Northeast Hospital in Humble, ½-mile south of Deerbrook Mall (FM 1960), just south of Tejas Toyota on the southbound feeder of US 59/I-69 in northeast Houston.

You can count on our best efforts, always. We go home gratified each day that we had the joy,

Because *health* is your greatest *wealth!*　　　　211

the honor, the privilege to help you *get out of your pain and get on with your life.*^{SM}

Now for the good news: Dr. T researches and probes daily to introduce newer, outstanding treatments. We never have a dull moment, always learning and preparing to make all of *your* moments *better and better!*

But maybe *your* problems are *different ...?*

Relax – most everyone is hesitant to get excited and hopeful when learning about a treatment they've never heard about before.

Yes, *we* know what conditions we help and about how much relief you can expect. We're one of the most qualified and respected offices in the country. We proudly share our experience with doctors around the country.

So ... rather than let this incredible opportunity slip through your hands, just do this now: **call us** with your questions: DIAL 1-800-FIX-PAIN.

Now is the time for you to pause – to close your eyes – to visualize how your life would look if you were to find true healing with unexpectedly wonderful results. With just a phone call, you could start to find out. Or maybe it's time for you to step forward and help your parents, your spouse, your adult children?

Find it *now* – Fix it *right!*

"I praise You, for I am fearfully and wonderfully made." Psalms 139:14

We have every reason to enjoy
when our patients find relief from their suffering
thanks to *our* commitment to
life *... celebrating health!*

Ebony – Lucrecia – Rena   Michelle – Cathy – Brooke
Dr. T

Dr. Trowbridge
humbly dedicates this book to
our wonderful patients
who, for almost 40 years,
have taught us so much
about illness and healing and about
Life ... ***Celebrating*** Health

Because *health* is your greatest *wealth!*

Pages I want to share with friends:

_____

_____

_____

_____

_____

_____

_____

_____

_____

_____

_____

_____

Proverbs 3:5-6: "Trust in the LORD with all your heart, and do not lean on your own understanding. In all your ways acknowledge Him, and He will make straight your paths."

You lose *every* time you don't try.ᔆᴹ

Find it *now* – Fix it *right!*

Sick and Tired?
is published by
Appleday Press
P. O. Box 60899 – Houston – Texas
ISBN 978-0-9990112-2-5
ebook pdf download ISBN 978-0-9990112-3-2
Copyright at Common Law 2017 John Parks Trowbridge
First Printing December 2017 – Printed in the United States of America

This book is **not** medical advice but presents only general information. Nothing in this book should be understood to offer specific treatment for **any** individual. Presented herein are unbiased facts, solely the professional medical opinions of the author. All reasonable care has been taken by the author to provide these details accurately, and he does not accept any responsibility or liability for any reliance on the material presented. **Discuss any questions with your diagnosing and treating physician**. No commercial funding or sponsorship was sought or provided. The U.S. Food and Drug Administration does not control diagnostic testing or drugs used in the practice of medicine, once they have been approved for general marketing. You must rely on the expertise, experience, and training of your treating physician for competent and meticulous care. You are encouraged to review sufficient educational materials to make a truly informed consent. Illustrations and photographs have been adapted from the public domain and are not known to be restricted from use in this publication.

Copies available:
DIAL 1-800-FIX-PAIN [349-7246]

Or order your copies from **amazon.com**

Feel free to make copies to share with your family, friends, coworkers, social club
Commercial reproduction or distribution or use in any way by any medical or health care provider or similar facility is expressly prohibited unless credit is clearly given to the author.

Learn about other life-saving programs:
Life Celebrating Health
has over 50 audio and video programs
DIAL 1-800-FIX-PAIN

www.healthCHOICESnow.com

You lose *every* time you don't try.ˢᵐ
Because *health* is your greatest *wealth!*

80200855R00119

Made in the USA
Lexington, KY
31 January 2018